LEVERAGE

CelebrityPress®
Winter Park, Florida

CONTENTS

CHAPTER 1

REVIEW YOUR GOALS DAILY

BY BRIAN TRACY

It is a psychological law that whatever we wish to accomplish
we must impress on the subjective or subconscious mind.
~ Orison Swett Marden

Sometimes I ask my audiences, "How many people here would like to double their incomes?" Not surprisingly, everyone raises his or her hand. I then go on to say, "Well, I have good news for you. Everybody here is going to double their income – guaranteed - if you *live* long enough!"

If your income increases at the rate of 3% to 4% per year, the average annual cost of living increase, you will double your income in about 20 years. But that is a long time to wait!

So the real question is not about doubling your income. The real question is, "How fast can you do it?"

DOUBLE THE SPEED OF GOAL ATTAINMENT

There are many techniques that can help you to achieve your personal and financial goals faster. In this chapter, I want to share with you a special method that has taken more people from rags to riches than any other single method ever discovered. It is simple, fast, effective and guaranteed to work – if you will practice it.

Earlier, I said, "You become what you think about, most of the time." This is the great truth that underlies all religion, philosophy, psychology and success. As a teacher of mine, John Boyle once said, "Whatever you can hold in your mind on a continuing basis, you can have." This is the key.

POSITIVE THINKING VERSUS POSITIVE KNOWING

Many people today talk about the importance of "positive thinking." Positive thinking is important, but it is not enough. Left undirected and uncontrolled, positive thinking can quickly degenerate into positive *wishing* and positive *hoping*. Instead of serving as an energy force for inspiration and higher achievement, positive thinking can become a little more than a generally cheerful attitude toward life, and whatever happens to you, positive or negative.

To be focused and effective in goal attainment, positive thinking must translate into "positive knowing." You must absolutely know and believe, in the depths of your being, that you are going to be successful at achieving a particular goal. You must proceed completely without doubt. You must be so resolute and determined, so convinced of your ultimate success, that nothing can stop you.

PROGRAM YOUR SUBCONSCIOUS MIND

Everything that you do to program your subconscious mind with this unshakeable conviction of success will help you achieve your goals faster. This method I am going to share with you can actually multiple your talents and abilities, and greatly increase the speed at which you move from wherever you are to wherever you want to go.

One of the important mental laws is, "Whatever is impressed, is expressed." Whatever you impress deeply into your subconscious mind will eventually be expressed in your external world. Your aim in mental programming is to impress your goals deeply into your subconscious mind so that they "lock in" and take on a power of their own. This method helps you to do that.

SYSTEMATIC VERSUS RANDOM GOAL SETTING

For many years, I worked away at my goals, writing them down once or twice a year and then reviewing them whenever I got a chance. Even this was enough to make an incredible difference in my life. Often, I would write down a list of goals for myself in January for the coming year. In December of that year, I would review my list and find that most of the goals had been accomplished, including some of the biggest and most unbelievable goals on the list.

I then learned the technique that changed my life. I discovered that if it is powerful for you to write down your goals once a year, it is even more powerful for you to write down your goals more often.

Some authors suggest that you write down and review your goals once a month, others once a week. What I learned was the power of writing and rewriting your goals *every single day.*

WRITE DOWN YOUR GOALS EACH DAY

Here is the technique. Get a spiral notebook that you keep with you at all times. Each day, open up your notebook and write down a list of your 10-15 most important goals, without referring to your previous list. Do this every day, day after day. As you do this, several remarkable things will happen.

The first day you write down your list of goals, you will have to give it some thought and reflection. Most people have never made a list of their 10 top goals in their entire lives.

The second day you write out your list, without reference to your previous list, it will be easier. However, your 10-15 goals will change, both in description and order of priority. Sometimes, a goal that you wrote one day will not appear the next day. It may even be forgotten and never reappear again. Or it may reappear later at a more appropriate time.

Each day that you write down your list of 10-15 goals, your definitions will become clearer and sharper. You will eventually find yourself writing down the same words every day. Your order of priority will also change as your life changes around you. But over time, after about 30 days, you will find yourself writing and rewriting the same goals every day.

YOUR LIFE TAKES OFF

And at about this time, something remarkable will happen in your life. It will take off! You will feel like a passenger in a jet hurtling down the runway. Your work and personal life will begin to improve dramatically. Your mind will sparkle with ideas and insights. You will start to attract people and resources into your life to help you to achieve your goals. You will start to make progress at a rapid rate, sometimes so fast that it will be a little scary. Everything will begin to change in a very positive way.

Over the years, I have spoken in 23 countries and addressed more than two million people. I have shared this "10 Goal Exercise" with hundreds of thousands of seminar participants. The exercise that I give them is a little simpler than the exercise that I am giving you here. Here it is.

I ask my audience members to make a list of 10 goals that they want to accomplish in the coming year. I tell them to put the list away for 12 months and then open it up. When they open up the list after a year, it will be as though a magic trick has been performed. In almost every case, eight out of their ten goals will have been accomplished, sometimes in the most remarkable ways.

I have given this exercise all over the world, to people in every language and culture. In virtually every case, when I return to their cities and countries, people line up to talk to me, like in a wedding receiving line, and tell me story after story about how their lives have changed after writing down their 10 goals a year or more ago.

PUTTING THIS METHOD TO WORK

In the exercise that we are discussing in this chapter, you will learn to get results that are far greater and far faster than those enjoyed by people who write their goals down only one time. Your results will double and triple and increase five and ten times as you use the same power of goal setting we have discussed earlier, but you will now be writing your goals down every day.

There are some special rules that you must follow to get the most out of this exercise. First, you must use the "Three 'P' Formula." Your goals must be written and described in the positive, present and personal tenses.

ACTIVATE YOUR SUBCONSCIOUS MIND

Your subconscious mind is only activated by affirmative statements phrased in the present tense. You therefore write down your goals as though you have *already* accomplished them. Instead of saying, "I will earn $50,000 in the next 12 months," you would say, "I earn $50,000 per year."

Your goals must be stated positively as well. Instead of saying, "I will quit smoking," or "I will lose a certain number of pounds of weight," you would say, "I am a non-smoker." Or, "I weigh X number of pounds." Your command must be positive because your subconscious mind cannot process a negative command. It is only receptive to a positive, present tense statement.

The third "P" stands for *personal*. From now on, and for the rest of your life, write out every goal beginning with the word "I," followed by a verb of some kind. You are the only person in the universe who can use the word "I" in relation to yourself. When your subconscious mind receives a command that begins with the word "I," it is as though the factory floor receives a production order from the head office. It goes to work immediately to bring that goal into your reality.

For example, you would not say, "My goal is to earn $50,000 per year." Instead, you would say, "I earn $50,000 per year." Begin each of your goals with phrases such as, "I earn, I weigh, I achieve, I win, I drive such and such a car, I live in a such and such a home, I climb such and such a mountain," and so on.

SET DEADLINES ON YOUR GOALS

To add power to your daily written goals, put a deadline at the end of each goal.

For example, you might write, "I earn an average of $5,000 per month by December 31st, (followed by a particular year)."

As we discussed in an earlier chapter, your mind loves deadlines and thrives on a "forcing system." Even if you do not know how the goal is going to be achieved, always give yourself a firm deadline. Remember, you can always change the deadline with new information. But be sure you have a deadline, like an exclamation point, after every goal.

HOW BADLY DO YOU WANT IT?

This exercise of writing out your 10 goals every single day is a test. The test is to determine how badly you really want to achieve these goals. Often you will write out a goal and then forget to write it down again. This simply means that you either don't really want to achieve that goal as much as something else, or you don't really believe that that goal is achievable for you.

However, the more you can discipline yourself to write and rewrite your goals each day, the clearer you will become about what you really want, and the more convinced you will become that it is possible for you.

TRUST THE PROCESS

When you begin writing your goals, you may have no idea how they will be accomplished. But this is not important. All that matters is that you write and rewrite them every day, in complete faith, knowing that every single time you write them down, you are impressing them deeper and deeper into your subconscious mind. At a certain point, you will begin to believe, with absolute conviction, that your goal is achievable.

Once your subconscious mind accepts your goals as commands from your conscious mind, it will start to make all your words and actions fit a pattern consistent with those goals. Your subconscious mind will start attracting into your life people and circumstances that can help you to achieve your goal.

YOUR MENTAL COMPUTER WORKS
24 HOURS PER DAY

Your subconscious mind works 24 hours a day, like a massive computer that is never turned off, to help bring your goals into reality. Almost without your doing anything, your goals will begin to materialize in your life, sometimes in the most remarkable and unexpected ways.

Some years ago, I met with a businessman in Los Angeles who had an absolutely ridiculous idea. He wanted to raise many millions of dollars in investment capital to create an amusement park in Hawaii that would be composed of restaurants, displays and exhibits from a variety of different countries from around the world. He was absolutely convinced that it would be a big attraction and that he could get the support and backing of all these different countries, as long as he could raise the startup money to launch the project.

In my youth and experience, I gently told him that I thought his idea was a complete fantasy. The complexity and expense of such a massive undertaking was so vast for a person of his limited resources that it would be a complete waste of time. I thanked him for his offer of a job in putting this whole plan together and politely departed.

This was in the 1960s. The next thing I heard about this project was that the Walt Disney Corporation had embraced it in its entirety, called it the "Experimental Prototype Community of Tomorrow (Epcot Center)," and had begun construction on it next to its Disneyland in Orlando, Florida. The amusement park and development has gone on to make hundreds of millions of dollars, year after year, and become one of the most popular tourist destinations in the world.

ACTIVATE ALL THE FORCES IN THE UNIVERSE

Here is the point. At that time, as a young man, I did not know that when you write down a goal, no matter how big or impossible it seems, you activate a series of forces in the universe that often make the impossible possible. I will explain this in great detail in the chapter on the "Superconscious Mind."

Whenever you write down a new goal of any kind, you may be skeptical and doubtful about the likelihood of accomplishing it. You may have the idea in your conscious mind, but you will have not yet developed the total belief and conviction that is possible for you. This is normal and natural. Don't let it stop you from using this method every day.

JUST DO IT!

All that is required to make this method work is for you to get a spiral notebook and then to discipline yourself each day to write down your 10 goals in the positive, present, personal tense. That's all you need. In a week, a month or a year, you will look around you and see that your whole life will have transformed in the most remarkable ways.

Even if you are skeptical about this method, it only requires about five minutes per day to try it out for yourself. The good news is that I have never met a person, in more than 20 years, who has ever told me that this method does not work. It is quite the opposite. I get letters, phone calls, emails and personal testimonials almost every day from people all over the country, and all over the world, whose lives have transformed so dramatically with this method as to be beyond belief!

MULTIPLY YOUR RESULTS

You can multiply the effectiveness of this method with a couple of additional techniques. First, after you have written down your goal in the positive, personal, present tense, write down at least three actions that you could take immediately to achieve that goal, also in the present, positive, personal tense.

For example, your goal could be to earn a certain amount of money. You could write, "I earn $50,000 dollars over the next 12 months." You could then write, immediately underneath:

1) I plan every day in advance.
2) I start in immediately on my most important tasks.
3) I concentrate single mindedly on my most important task until it is complete.

Whatever your goal, you can easily think of three action steps that you can take immediately to achieve that goal. When you write down the action steps, you program them into your subconscious mind along with the goal.

At a certain point, you will find yourself actually taking the steps that you wrote down, sometimes without even thinking about it. And each step you take will move you more rapidly toward your ultimate objective.

USE 3 X 5 INDEX CARDS

Another way that you can increase the effectiveness of daily goal setting is by transferring your goals to 3 x 5 index cards. Write one goal on each card in large letters. Carry these cards with you at all times. Whenever you have a few spare moments, take out your index cards and review your goals, one by one.

Each of these goals should be written as a personal, positive, present tense affirmation. Someone once said, "I would rather a morning without breakfast than a morning without affirmations." Each time you use these cards, take a few moments, breathe deeply and relax, and then review each of your goals, one at a time.

As you read the goal to yourself, imagine the goal as though it were already a reality. Actually see yourself at the goal, enjoying the goal, feeling the pleasure of having achieved the goal.

Alternately, as you read your index cards, you can imagine specific steps that you can take immediately to achieve that goal. You should actually imagine yourself taking those steps. Then relax, and go on to the next goal.

Ideally, you should review your goals on index cards twice per day. Read them once in the morning before you start off and once in the evening before you go to bed. You can also carry them around with you and review them during the day, whenever you have a few spare moments.

THE BEST TIMES FOR MENTAL PROGRAMMING

There are two times of the day that are ideal for writing and rewriting your goals, and for reading and reviewing your index cards. These are: the last thing in the evening, before you go to bed, and the first thing in the morning, before you start off.

When you rewrite and review your goals in the evening, you program them into your subconscious mind. Your subconscious mind then has an opportunity to work on your goals all night long while you are sleeping. You will often arise with wonderful ideas for things to do or people to call to help you achieve your goals.

When you rewrite and review your goals in the morning, before you start off, you set yourself up for positive thinking and positive acting all day long. Just as physical exercise in the morning warms up your physical body and muscles, reviewing your goals in the morning warms up your mind and prepares you to be at your very best throughout the day.

The sum total result of rewriting and reviewing your goals each day, morning and evening, is that you will impress them ever more deeply into your subconscious mind. You will gradually move from positive *thinking* to positive *knowing*. You will develop a deep and unshakeable conviction that your goals are attainable, and that it is only a matter of time before you achieve them, and you will be right.

Review Your Goals Daily:

1. Get yourself a spiral notebook this very day and write down 10-15 goals that you would like to achieve in the foreseeable future.

2. Create a set of 3x5 index cards with your goals written out in the positive, personal, present tense to carry with you wherever you go.

3. Visualize and imagine your goals as they would be when you have achieved them each night before you go to sleep.

4. Think of three things you could do to achieve each of your goals. Always think in terms of specific actions you could take.

5. Discipline yourself to rewrite your goals every day, without reviewing your previous list, until you become absolutely convinced that achieving your goals is inevitable.

About Brian

Brian Tracy is one of the top business experts and trainers in the world. He has taught more than 5,000,000 salespeople in 80 countries.

Brian is the President of Brian Tracy International, committed to teaching ambitious individuals how to rapidly increase their sales and personal incomes.

CHAPTER 2

BY PERSONAL INTRODUCTION ONLY

BY PAUL MARTIN

THE GREAT PYRAMIDS

They are ancient engineering marvels so impressive that their very existence tell you all you need to know about the human ability to dream, execute, and problem-solve. Constructed over 4,500 years ago, the Great Pyramid of Giza is the oldest of the Seven Wonders of the Ancient World and the only one to remain largely intact.

It is estimated 2.3 million stone blocks were used in its construction, each weighing an average of 2.5 to 15 tons while the largest granite stones were 25 to 80 tons. Yet, the Egyptians not only moved the massive stones into place to build the pyramids, some to a truly amazing height of 481 feet, but they also moved the granite stones 500 miles from a quarry in Aswan and carved them to perfection with only rudimentary tools.

How in the world did they do all that?

Even today scientists can't really be sure how they were built, and without the benefit of cell phone cameras, TikTok or

Facebook with which to record and share this engineering feat, the Egyptians left us only their finished masterpieces and the inspiration and awe they inspire. One can only surmise that their desire to achieve such a tribute to their higher power must have dramatically outweighed their insecurities.

Much like the builders of the great pyramids with their rudimentary tools and strong desire, I perfected a client acquisition system which I called "The Wheel of Life," leveraging relationship and reputational marketing to build a strong client base using one extremely basic tool, the personal introduction. In hindsight, I should have called it The Wheel of Plenty or Abundance, because that is exactly what it turned out to be – as many great clients as you want.

Where did this all start? Well, this was when I left the UK Royal Air Force (RAF) and became a financial advisor.

What a challenge, how was I to achieve success? Now when I look back it seems a little like the feat of building the great pyramids, but the difference was they knew what they were doing, and I had no idea. We had to find our own clients which they told me was called "prospecting," and I was trained in cold calling/cold contact methods. I suppose because of the high rejection cold methods bring, it is a little like prospecting for gold – where you are lucky if you find anything – hence the expression "prospecting." I did not like the cold processes, and it felt like moving heavy stones but without the leverage the ancient Egyptians had.

I had to find leverage. I just knew there had to be a better way than hearing no, no, no. With no leverage, just sweat and tears with few wins and lots of rejections, it was hard at times to keep going. One co-worker suggested the business telephone directory, but explained his unique twist was instead of starting at 'A' and working to 'Z' like everyone else, he started at 'Z' and worked back to 'A'. There's got to be a better way than that, I thought, but thanked him for his insight.

Then I got my first break. Angus Stott, an experienced sales manager, and I sometimes shared a car to the office as we lived in the same town. He said, "You look as though you are serious about this business." and handed me a book and said, "When I first started, someone gave me this book and I now want you to have it, and I hope it helps you as it did me." I thanked him enthusiastically and could not wait to get home and start reading.

Then I got my first client, Shawn Healy, who worked with me in the RAF. Proudly, I took my first sale to the office – where at a meeting I was expecting applause, but all I got was laughter – when the manager explained to everyone that he calculated my commission would not cover my gasoline. He said if I had sold a different policy I would have earned ten times more, so I would not last long in this business. I replied, "If I have to do what you say to be successful then yes, I will not last long in this business, but I would like to see where you all are in three years and where I am."

The second break came from something in the book given to me by Angus. I read how after getting a new client you should get them to write something on the back of one of your business cards to show to someone who the client may know. Now I did not see this as my leverage but as a step in the right direction. I gave it some considerable thought then, wow, I came up with an idea. I could go one better than a note, I could write a letter for the clients to sign and ask them for someone specifically I could give it to that they knew. As I now had about ten clients, I made a list of them all, called this list "My Top 10 for Starters" and decided to approach them. Top of the list was Ian and Caryn Harrison who had Life Assurance Policies with me.

I rang and arranged to visit them. The day came and I began to get extremely nervous. Why, they were clients, they trusted me but I was so very nervous. I got there over an hour early to be sure not to be late and sat in my automobile around the corner, my palms sweating, worrying even more until the time came.

"Hello Paul, come in," said Ian and Caryn, "sit down, what is this all about?" Ur...umm...er...well, it's about umm...you probably don't want to but maybe...er...umm...I waffled on not knowing what I was going to say – no plan, no idea just nervous, very nervous – by now fearing they would throw me out and cancel all their policies with me. Why was I risking this, I thought. Caryn, stood up and I thought, here we go, and she said sorry but she had to go and sort out some washing upstairs.

I stammered on to Ian, not making clear my intentions holding my blank letters of introduction in my hand until Ian said: "Paul, are you asking us to introduce your services to others we know?" Fearing the absolute worst, I reluctantly said yes. Ian jumped up...oh no, my heart sank. He went to the bottom of the stairs and called, "Caryn, Caryn come down here." I was reaching for my briefcase already, Caryn came downstairs quickly. Ian said excitedly, "you know the other day we were speaking about how we could introduce Paul to our friends but was nervous about asking him. Well, he has a professional system to do just that, isn't it great, just great." "Yes" said Caryn, coming to sit down again. "We have four close friends we want you to help just like you have helped us. We have spoken to them already and they want you to call, but we did not know if you would be happy with this."

I was just speechless. I didn't know what to say so I just nodded, but then I realized what a momentous moment this was. It felt like one of those Indiana Jones films where at the right time of day, the sun beams in a streak of golden light and triggers secret chambers to open, revealing rooms full of gold. I had my leverage. Small effort, big movement.

As I happily skipped (walked really) down the garden path back to my automobile, I made a resolve never to cold call or use the yellow pages again. I have been developing and perfecting this system since 1989, including the timing, as a few months later I made it work before someone was even a client. Yes, I was being introduced at initial exploratory meetings, so even if they did not become a client, I had a meeting and replaced it with at least one meeting, usually more, until I was regularly booking weeks ahead. I designed a script so I knew what I was going to say every time, and I could review it and improve it. In the end, just like two parts of hydrogen and one part of oxygen make water every time, I too had a scientific formula that worked. Now everything was different. I was top of the sales board, and everyone wanted to know my secret.

Within six weeks I was a team leader, then three months later I was asked to move to the firm's elite secret salesforce, where in just a few months I was in the top ten financial advisers nationally. Just over a year after leaving the RAF, I had quadrupled my income, had a company car (my first-ever new car) and travelling home one evening on the A47 in England, my mobile phone rang. (Anyone remembers those Motorola bricks?) A voice said: "Hello Paul, I know you are happy where you are, successful and don't speak to recruitment agencies, but we have something in common which means you must give me one minute of your time right now – My name is Phillip, and my surname is also Martin."

Intrigued, I said "OK, let me pull over." He went on to tell me a lot about myself and my fascination in using technology in the sales process, how I worked "by personal introduction only" and about this new exciting sales force who wanted to make me – yes me – a full manager on salary, override,…the lot. It would double my current earnings overnight to eight times what I earned only fifteen months earlier in the RAF. They had the technology and wanted me because I worked "by personal introduction only."

So, because of my leveraging personal introductions, I was now a sales manager and had to recruit a sales team. How was I going to do this? I thought, is this so different from selling? No, well, personal introductions it is then. Among others, I turned again to Shawn Healy who introduced me to Jim Boomer, who in turn introduced Robin West (who has been one of my very best friends for more than 30 years now), and Shawn, who, if you remember my co-workers laughed at me for selling a policy for his needs, not mine, cashed in that very policy to give himself early cashflow so he could join my team as well!

I recruited more of us, became the manager of the top team, branch, then region, with the best productivity in the history of the company, and I got promotion after promotion because the financial advisers all used my personal introduction system. It works in numerous different sectors and is successful for every operator who uses it because they work "by personal introduction only." The system has evolved and is still as effective as it was then. In March 2020, because of the pandemic and so many people had to work from home, I tweaked it and added it to an online video meeting system, so that no one in my organization, or any of those I mentor, faced any drop in income whatsoever. In fact, they are even busier than they were before, but keeping themselves and clients safe by working remotely.

The system has not changed substantially in over 30 years. What has changed is the number of people who have met and exceeded their personal sales and financial goals using the system I developed.

You might be thinking, "Paul, what does all that mean to me?" My experience - both failures and successes - helped me leave footprints in the sand for you to follow so you can achieve your goals with better, faster results. But how?

I'm nearer to the end of my career than the beginning now, and if I am honest, I have not shared externally what I learned. I'd like one of my pyramids I leave for future generations to be my experience with personal introductions. There are other foundation stones which complement the system that helps any salesperson or those in business build an empire.

1. Put others First

I put Shawn first, I thought only of him and what he wanted rather than me and look at what I achieved by doing so?

I always say to those I mentor: The degree to which you will be truly successful will be in direct proportion to the degree to which you are unselfish.

2. Add Value and Leverage Personal Introductions

Always seek to add value in any given situation and try to "give more than you get." Communicate information of value WITHOUT COST OR COMMITMENT so the customer is in a better place to make a decision when the time comes. Before any close, speak about how you have helped them and directly afterwards, before any sale takes place, ask them to introduce you to others. A salesperson or businessperson rarely leverages an introduction at this point in the process, so be very different. You may have asked yourself the question, "How can I reach more people, faster, with better results?"

If you close three out of every four personal introductions, what is more important to you? The sale in front of you or four new personal introductions?

3. Read and constantly learn all you can

As Brian Tracy says, never stop learning, always look to develop and learn more. Try to work on yourself. In a trade organisation, I know they require twenty-four hours of Continuous Practice Development (CPD) a year. I believe business is 5% technical knowledge, and 95% skills, methods and systems. Now, you must know 100% of the 5%, that is very important, but what about the 95% if 5% is 24 hours? Well, it is 480 hours a year (which is 40 hours a month), or over a 48-week year allowing for holidays equals ten hours every single week? If you worked on yourself, your skills, systems and methods for ten hours a week where would you be in just one year?

Read, listen to programs, think and plan strategically, ask for help, meet with peers, invest time and work on yourself. My success is in no small part due to working on myself. As Brian said in the original "Taking Charge of Your Life" – "If it's to be, it's up to me, if it's to be, it's up to you…"

4. Work hard

The elevator to success is out of order, but the stairs are always available. Arrive early, stay late, and Brian Tracy says, "When you work, work."

5. Borrow Credibility and Trust

With personal introductions, you borrow the credibility and the trust of the person who is making the introduction. By extension, you are now credible and trusted to a certain degree by the referral. What we have found over many years is that people like doing business by personal introduction – just like I found out by accident with Caryn and Ian Harrison all those years ago. Personal introductions also question the price less, buy more, buy again and are over 85% more likely to introduce you to others.

6. Teach them to fish

Companies are often trying to provide leads for their salespeople, but if you feed people, they eat for a day whereas if you teach people to fish, they feed themselves.

7. Engage Warm Leads Only

Most companies are used to telling a client how they're going to communicate with them. They send sales flyers, marketing emails, call at times inconvenient to them with automated phone bots, etc. Well, the client nowadays wants to be able to choose the who, when and how they connect with a company. The customer wants to be in control. They can only be reached if they want you to reach them. Note that there are regulations in many countries regarding contacting people.

Another great advantage is that by working exclusively by personal introduction, none of the above applies because the prospect has already given permission for you to contact them.

8. Rely Upon Social Proof

Their friend has introduced them, and their friend got introduced by somebody else. So, therefore, this is normal and natural for the client to introduce others. It's a great way of doing business because you're already in front of them because of someone they trust. People like to do business with those they know, like and trust.

9. Birds of a feather flock together

Once you have a client who is a good fit for you, it is likely the people they introduce will also be a good fit. Think about your circle of friends and family, how are they similar to you? Not necessarily in character but circumstances such as relationship type, age, children of similar ages, interests, hobbies, homeowner or not, whether they own a business or are employed, etc.

10. Best of all – it's free

Personal introductions are 100% FREE…

11. You can't hit the ball if you don't swing at it!

~ Baseball analogy

I'm not saying the system works 100% of the time, but if you use it 100% of the time, it will work more times than not and that is enough to make you wealthy. The top person I mentored in 2021 is turning over around $320,000 a year on their own by personal introductions only, no sales team. Mr. Jean Lagadec, my longest-serving mentoree, retired in 2019 after 22 years with me after building a client bank of 2,400 annual re-occurring income clients all exclusively by personal introductions only. Working by Personal Introductions also allowed Jean the time to develop as a successful professional artist.

Personal introductions is not merely a business system; it becomes a way of life. I ask people I know, like, trust and respect for personal introductions for nearly everything I do or buy. Personal introductions have allowed me to emigrate from the UK way back in 2007 first to Spain, and we are now splitting our time between Poland and Egypt where we have built bespoke homes. I don't just mean earning money as my building contacts, contractors, suppliers, furniture makers, etc. were all personally introduced to me, as were those who kindly let a 58-year-old hobble around the football pitch.

Granted, this system isn't for everyone. You need to develop the inner strength to do the mental heavy lifting, but this is learnable and the great news is as Brian Tracy says, "You are not born with skills, you can learn and develop skills," just like I did.

It all begins with a simple decision, perseverance, and the willingness to use the tools you already have at your disposal. Find your leverage to build your pyramid that will stand the test of time.

Dedication

To our beloved mother, Ethne Martin, who was taken from my brother Ian Martin O.B.E. and me tragically when we were so young. Anything good about me has come from my mum. I believe she must be looking down on us as rarely do two brothers achieve so much in such different walks of life – so thank you, mum. Also to our Auntie Dolores, our mother's sister, who has never tired of helping us to know our mother and who she was, Thank you, Auntie.

About Paul

Paul is happiest when he is with his wife Jolanta, daughters and grandchildren. After emigrating from the UK in 2007 first to Spain, you can now find Paul either at their smallholding in West Pomerania, Poland, an area of outstanding natural beauty known for forests, lakes and wildlife (including rare wild European Bison) or on the shores of The Red Sea, Hurghada, Egypt where they also have a home.

When Paul is not keeping busy at work, with his family or playing football, he and Jolanta enjoy growing tomatoes and other food, spending time with their sheep, pony, pigs, chickens or milking their goats for milk and homemade cheese during the very hot Polish summers, or relaxing during the winter in Egypt, swimming, snorkeling and where Paul, even at 58, plays football (more slowly nowadays) two or three times a week. Paul is also known for the authentic paella he learned to make while in Spain, he even imports rice from Valencia and saffron from La Mancha.

Professional Purpose:
What gets Paul up in the morning is his passion to help others and be of value every single day by striving to share his vision and inspire others to achieve for themselves.

Paul is always looking to grow, learn and develop, and he believes in Brian Tracy's mantra that lifelong continuous learning is one of the major keys to success. To that end, Paul has decided to become more visible in 2021 by co-authoring this book, which is his first of a series, and by launching new, exciting, entrepreneurial businesses for tomorrow:

1. **The Brian Tracy International Clubs** *by Paul Martin* –
   (www.bti.club & email: paul@bti.club)
   Paul was introduced to Brian Tracy's materials in 1989 and credits Brian with changing both his life and those he has mentored. A member of Brian's inner circle and owner of several of Brian's corporate programs, Paul is proud and excited to have been trusted by Brian Tracy International to start a new exclusive concept in personal and corporate development. It will use a first-of-its-kind mobile App with Omni-channel persistent communication to digitally get better results much faster.

2. Style Assessments

Before mass remote working, which Paul believes is here to stay, we recruited those who were suited to work in an office environment and enjoyed the company of others, but now the situation is completely different. A person who is task-oriented may be a better fit in the new hybrid world of home and office working? Style Assessments helps you identify good fits, and by understanding your style, become a better communicator, leader or team member in the new normal.

3. Digli™ (www.digli.co.uk)

Office in your pocket, Omni-communication mobile App for professionals to navigate effectively the new digital world of hybrid and office working. Be where your clients already are to improve their customer experience a hundred times over.

4. ID-entity™ (www.id-entity.co.uk)

A simple, slick, smart digital identification App for professionals who are required to verify a customer's ID, reduce risk, and save time and money by being AML complaint. It will improve customer experience whilst reducing their frustration with unreliable manual processes.

5. The Millionaire WillWriter

Since 1992, Paul's proprietary systems for WillWriters have helped himself and others build extremely successful WillWriting businesses. Until now only his exclusive inner circle has been allowed to use these systems. The Millionaire WillWriter will allow members access to Paul's materials.

CHAPTER 3

LEVERAGING AN INDUSTRY EXPERT TO BE MORE PROFITABLE!

BY KEVIN HODES

Ok, you have done your research, and you think you have the best deal for accepting credit cards. You signed up, you are processing for a few months, and you realize that it is not what you were told or thought it would be when you look over your statement. Well, let me tell you, you are not alone. It is time to leverage over 20 years of knowledge and expertise to help you be as profitable as you can be. Let's get started!

There are a few factors to look for when considering credit card processing. But first, please stop doing the following:

- Stop taking the calls from telemarketers! There is no such thing as wholesale pricing, and none of these people are with Visa or MasterCard. It sure does sound good, doesn't it?

- Stop signing up with anyone that just walks in off the street! Cold calling representatives typically are still new to the industry. They most likely do not have the knowledge and or experience to possibly set you up correctly. Ever hear, let me call my manager to see if we can get you a better deal? They

35

are calling in to get advice on what to do next. Next thing you know, you are speaking with the hard closing manager.

- Stop calling organizations that send you postcards and letters in the mail! These are your typical bait and switch teaser rates. Where are these companies anyway?

- Square, PayPal, Stripe, and QuickBooks pricing strategies can be the most expensive! The big box stores would never use these options. Why would you?

Now that we have covered the slimy part of credit card processing and I have your attention. There are two components of credit card processing, price, and service. It is hard to get both, but when you do, latch onto that company or salesperson because they are few and far between. Anyone can undercut another organization for a penny here or there, but if there is no service, who are you calling when you have a problem. Or you can have the best service but the worst price. Have you ever heard the saying:

"Price, Quality, or Service? Choose Two!"

What if I told you that you can have all three? With a little research, you can leverage the knowledge you are about to learn and get Price, Quality, and Service.

So, how do you get the best deal? First, look for an organization that has been referred to you by another business owner that you know. Companies that have been around a long time and have built their clientele from mostly all referrals probably means that they are doing something right. If you have been in business for a few years, you most likely have been burned already with promises from shady salespeople. Remember this, just like you, there are experts in all fields of business, and not all organizations are the same even though they may offer the same product. Find a Certified Payment Professional. Yes, there is such a person. There is a registry, and you can search for someone in your area. Or work with a credit card processor that has been endorsed by an association that you pay dues to. That organization has done extensive research to make sure you are getting the best deal and will not be taken advantage of.

If you are thinking your bank may be a great way to get a merchant account, banks do not process credit cards. They have contracts with processors and can have as much as a 40% markup. Banks are great at offering a checking account, maybe a mortgage, or giving a bank loan. But do not fall for the story that you have to switch your credit card processing if you want a loan from their bank. Just tell them no. Do you think they are going to give you great service because you deposit monies in their bank? They will refer you to the 800 number when you need help. They cannot even see your merchant account at the branch, so how are they going to help you? They will be happy to take your deposit if you have one or pay that loan payment.

Did you know that when you are sitting with the banker, and they put that strange screen over the computer, it is designed to give them the questions to ask you so they receive points or bonuses that can equal as much as $500 just for referring you to other services within the bank, specifically the credit card processing? So, who are they helping, you or themselves? It is not the banker's fault; it's what the big banks teach them to do.

Beware of software providers or distributors that say they have a preferred vendor. Or they will give you a discounted price on the product you are buying if you use their preferred vendor to process your credit cards. Ever wonder why they do that? The software organization or distributor will then make a piece of the action. Typically, it is a sizable markup. It is 40% more than you would pay if you were with a company that is thinking about your profit instead of their own. This is now a source of income, and they have locked you in so you can never switch, although they always guarantee you have the best deal. But I am not sure how paying 40% more is the best deal?

Work with an organization that does not lock you into using their preferred vendor! It opens the door for competition, and it keeps everyone honest. You should be able to do your research, negotiate, and switch when you want. Yes, research the company that you are considering. Preferred does not always mean it is in your best interest. In this case, preferred really means what is in their best interest.

Another important factor, PCI DSS is real! Or better known as, The Payment Card Industry Data Security Standard. And, if you do not get compliant, the processors will charge you a monthly non-compliance fee. I have seen this as high as $159 per month! You should be leery of your current or any future processor if they say that they will not charge you or say you do not have to become compliant. Everyone *must get compliant*, and there are systems in place that cost money to be there to help you with this process. You can google PCI DSS and see for yourself how important it is to get compliant. Remember, you are a consumer as well, and this is to help stop fraud.

A few years ago, a longtime customer called me and said, 'Get down here right away'. I was happy to show up as I always do, and he and his wife proceeded with letting me know that we had been charging them more than they should have been paying for years. I was shocked because we are aggressively priced, so our customers are not paying more than they should. They stated that this very nice person had just left and was from Visa and MasterCard and said they needed new credit card equipment for $59 per month, and they would save thousands of dollars the moment they switched to this wholesale pricing.

Remember I said earlier there is no such thing as wholesale pricing or merchant salespeople with Visa and Mastercard? They handed me the new offer to review. First, I stated, you do not need new equipment, and if you do, we will upgrade it at our cost, not yours. Spending $59 per month for a 48-month, non-cancelable lease is not necessary. Never lease a credit card machine. Companies that care about you and not themselves will offer equipment to use for as long as you are a customer. If your current processor does not do that, find one that does.

I continued to review and stated, "The new rates being offered would increase your fees 40%. You will now be leasing a credit card machine that we have always provided at our cost, and you will pay more in processing fees every month." They said that they have it in writing that there will be a guarantee of savings from this nice person and they said we need this new equipment because it is out of compliance. There was nothing I could do at this time, so I left and requested the closure of the merchant account.

Fast forward two years, I received a call, and they said they made a terrible mistake and needed help. They realized several months after moving away from us that they were paying 50% more in fees and called the company that signed them up. The nice person that had signed them up two years ago was no longer with the company, and they cannot return the non-cancelable 48-month leased credit card machine.

Several months passed, and they were called upon by another company on the phone that said they could fix all their issues and just happened to be in the area. This new nice person also offered lower rates and said they needed a new credit card machine that would work with a special system that no one else offered. I figured out that these new rates did not change, and the new credit card machine was proprietary and was another 48-month non-cancelable lease. At this point, they were frantic, and that is why they called me.

I gave them some advice, and they are back working with us. This is a true story of one of our customers being taken advantage of. I was so disappointed that someone in my industry had taken advantage of a business owner in this way that I decided to drive to the address on the business card of the second company. It was a fictitious address. This happens every day to business owners all over the country looking for a better deal. It is important to know that most processors will meet or beat any deal you receive if it is not a bait and switch offer. There are professionals in all fields of business. Some are better than others. If you do not have your very own professional credit card person, you may be paying more than you should and may not be receiving the service you deserve. Or worse, you may think all the people in credit card processing are all the same. I can honestly say there are good people in credit card processing industry; they can just be hard to find.

Now, for the part you have been really waiting for. How do I get the best rates? First, stop shopping by rate! That sounds crazy, doesn't it? Well, when you shop by rate, you may get a lower rate, but other fees will be charged elsewhere to make up the difference. It is a numbers game, and you will always lose with this buying process. And salespeople will take full advantage of you, knowing you are the company looking for the cheapest deal. The cheapest deal can be the most expensive.

Ok, here is a secret I want you to know. Take your total fees deducted and divide that into your total credit cards processed. This will give you your aggregate rate. The factors of your aggregate increasing and decreasing monthly will depend on how you accept and process credit cards. Swiped, chipped, contactless, over the phone, internet, average ticket, and what type of cards you receive. Swiped, chipped, and contactless will be the most cost-effective; internet and hand-keyed are typically the most expensive.

To keep your aggregate low, you need to work with a company that agrees to the Interchange plus pricing model. Interchange is the cost the card issuer has established for that exact credit card. There are hundreds of these different rates. Yes, hundreds and they range from 0.05% to 3.25%. But, if you have interchange plus, it will hit the network, and you will always get the best price for that exact card type no matter if you swipe, chip, tap, hand key, or it is processed on your website.

Stay clear of tiered or bundled rate structures. Let me explain. Tiered and bundled rates may make it easier for you to understand the fees, but they are not cost effective for you. In this retail face-to-face debit card scenario, your current processor set your tiered rate at 1.59%, but when it hit the processing network, we know the cost is actually 0.05%. In this tiered scenario, why would you want to pay 1.54% more? In this retail face-to-face debit card scenario, your current processor set your bundled rate at 2.75%, but when it hit the processing network, we know the cost is actually 0.05%. In this bundled scenario, you would pay 2.70% more! Why would you want a bundled rate? This is simple math, and there is no need to pay more when you should not have to.

In the past, the Interchange pricing model has been reserved for large national merchants. It is now available to you and is by far the fairest pricing model. In this pricing model, interchange and assessments are passed directly to the merchant, with a separate fee added for profit. The merchant always knows where the actual profit is. There are no hidden fees or surprises. Interchange is always the way to go; you do not want to be on the tiered or bundled rate structures.

After you have met or spoken with that new individual and or new company, get on the internet and do a Google search of that company and salesperson. See what others are saying. Did you just find out the person you have been talking with and is getting ready to handle your income was working at a big box store last year? Did the company they represent have a PO Box? C'mon man, are you crazy? Go to the BBB and find out if they have complaints. Find the expert. But how do you find an expert? An expert is somebody who has broad and deep competence in terms of knowledge, skill, and experience through practice and education in a particular field. They have recognized credentials and a proven track record.

Experts in the credit card processing industry can be very difficult to find. That is why you should contact other business owners and ask for a referral to an agent or company that has worked with their business for at least ten years or more. And talk with two or three other businesses for a referral. I hate to say it, but would you trust a financial planner that has not been in their industry for at least ten years? The best deal and service after the sale can be found through a little research and a qualified referral.

Seriously, when it comes to your money, DO YOUR RESEARCH, then leverage that knowledge. If it sounds too good to be true, it probably is.

- For more information, visit: www.Swypit.com, or call 1-877-379-9748.

About Kevin

Since 1999, owner and founder of Swypit, Kevin Hodes, prides himself on bringing honesty and integrity to the world of credit card processing. Swypit provides much more than just a service. Swypit takes great pride in assisting their clients with growing and managing their business while directly and successfully contributing to their client's profitability. His expertise in the merchant service industry is sought out, and he has been seen on ABC, NBC, CBS, A&E, E! and Bravo networks.

In an industry that is rife with third-party providers who are often more intent upon selling equipment than providing an effective solution for your business, Swypit ensures that their clients feel like more than just a number and receive an unparalleled level of communication and customer support.

Swypit provides world-class service, rates, and leading-edge technology. In addition, they offer businesses free credit card terminals, assistance with point-of-sale systems capable of managing inventory, payroll, gift cards, as well as cash advance services. They also offer surcharging with no-cost credit card processing.

Kevin Hodes is a three-time Best-Selling Author and Executive Producer of the following documentaries:

- *Maximum Achievement: The Brian Tracy Story*
- *The Jay Abraham Story: Getting Everything You Can Out Of All You've Got*
- *Folds of Honor: A Fighter Pilot's Mission to Deliver Healing and Hope to America*

Kevin has received numerous Telly awards, and most recently, *Folds of Honor* received two Emmys.

Staying active in the community and giving back is important to Kevin, which is why direct profits from Swypit go back into many community organizations, with his primary focus being *The American Fallen Soldiers Project* and *The Folds of Honor.*

CHAPTER 4

LEVERAGE ACTIVE LISTENING TO BOOST YOUR RELATIONSHIPS
3 KEYS TO AVOID COMMUNICATION ERRORS

BY CLIFTON HOLDEN

Half a league, half a league,
Half a league onward,
All in the valley of Death
  Rode the six hundred.
"Forward, the Light Brigade!
Charge for the guns!" he said.
Into the valley of Death
  Rode the six hundred.[1]

Alfred Lord Tennyson's *The Charge of the Light Brigade* retells the deadly tragedy of the British troops who were largely mown down in their attempt to execute an order to 'advance rapidly to the front,' even though the issuing Commander, Lord Raglan, had intended the message to direct an attack on a completely different target.

---

1. https://www.poetryfoundation.org/poems/45319/the-charge-of-the-light-brigade

The Light Brigade memorialized in Tennyson's poem fought for the British against the Russians during the Crimean War, in the battle of Balaclava, October 25, 1854. The infamous charge became a source of controversy in Victorian England, as officers present that day continued to argue, even until the grave, over which commander bore fault in the tragedy.

THREE TYPES OF COMMUNICATION ERRORS TO AVOID

Examining historical accounts of the day, we can see the impacts of several types of miscommunication on the ill-fated charge. Experts tell us there are three types of communication errors:

1. Errors of Transmission
2. Errors of Reception
3. Errors of Context, or Perspective

In the case of the Light Brigade, examples of all three types of errors can be found. The original order from Raglan was written on a slip of paper and handed to a junior officer known for his impulsive and insubordinate nature, a certain Captain Nolan. Nolan was charged with delivering the message from Raglan, who was up on a bluff overlooking the battle, down to Lord Lucan, commanding his forces on the plain below.

The message read: *"Ld. Raglan wishes the cavalry to advance rapidly to the front - follow the enemy and try to prevent the enemy carrying away the guns. Troop Horse artillery may accompany. French cavalry is on your left. Immediate!"*

Before writing his barely intelligible order to the Commander of the Light Brigade, Raglan had just enjoyed seeing his Heavy Cavalry route a Russian artillery position above the plain of battle. Hoping to ensure the enemy did not return to reinforce the position and reclaim the heavy battery of guns from which they had been forced to retreat, Raglan intended the Light Brigade to follow the Heavy Cavalry's earlier maneuver.

1.   Errors of transmission

However, due to the unclear nature of Raglan's own message, the first communication error was committed. This initial error of transmission: the general lack of clarity in the written order, was compounded by the way the order was delivered. Raglan selected his best horseman, Captain Nolan, to deliver the urgent message.

The hot-headed Nolan took the message and charged his steed down to deliver the order to Commander of the Cavalry, Lord Lucan. The historian Christopher Hibbert notes that Lucan and Nolan detested each other, a fact which was known to Raglan. Further, Raglan knew Nolan to be impetuous and often insubordinate but felt speed of delivery trumped considerations of character.

2.   Errors of reception

As Lucan read the message slowly, 'with much consideration — perhaps consternation would be the better word — at once seeing its impracticability for any useful purpose whatever'. He urged 'the uselessness of such an attack and the danger attending it'.

Seeing Lucan rereading the note again as if to search for some reprieve, Nolan became angry. 'Lord Raglan's orders are that the cavalry should attack immediately.'

The initial errors of transmission: the imprecise directive and the untrustworthy messenger, were now being met by errors of reception, as Lucan's instinct to ask for clarification was being overruled. Lucan gave in to the perceived urgency of the situation by failing to demand that Nolan return to Raglan for clearer instructions.

3.   Errors of context, or perspective

'Attack, sir! Attack what? What guns, sir? Where and what to do?' Commander Lucan famously replied, referencing the third in the complement of errors, a great error of perspective.

From Raglan's elevated position, it was clear to see the elevated gun placement that the heavy cavalry had just routed. But on the plain below, no such perspective was available, and the only guns visible to Nolan and Raglan were the reinforced gun placement at the front of the Russian line, over a mile away, with artillery and heavy gun placements on either side.

'There, my Lord!' Nolan swung his arms out and appeared to indicate the far front of the battlefield. 'There is your enemy! There are your guns!' Leaving Lucan without clarification, Nolan trotted away to join the line of cavalry for the impending charge.

The only guns visible to Lucan were those at the end of the valley where the Russian cavalry was also stationed. With his presumption of the target reinforced and pressured by the impetuous Nolan, Lucan made up his mind to order the attack. He trotted over to the unit commander, Lord Cardigan, and gave the order. Cardigan replied, 'Certainly, Sir. But allow me to point out to you that the Russians have a battery in the valley in our front, and batteries and riflemen on each flank.'

'I know it,' replied Lucan. 'But Lord Raglan will have it. We have no choice but to obey.'

As the men of the Light Brigade bravely took up their positions to charge, they saw in front of them over a mile of reinforced enemy ground to charge through. Of the 600 men in that unit, fewer than half survived the initial charge, with most gunned down by cannon fire.

A TRAGEDY OF MISCOMMUNICATION

Valiant as the men of the brigade were that day, the famous series of miscommunications that led to the charge became symbolic of the inadequacies of the British officer corps. Ultimately stemming from the events of that day, the entire system of recruitment for officers was changed to address a culture of petty grievance and imprecision that led to the tragic and apparently needless deaths of the men in the Light Brigade.

But what can we learn today from the tragedy described by Tennyson in *The Charge of the Light Brigade*?
With better communication:

— more careful and specific choices in transmission,
— more rigor in reception
— by eliminating the errors of perspective with additional context, many deaths could have been avoided

Today, coaches have access to a number of active listening techniques that can help us to avoid these types of communication errors, which have the potential to be personally devastating. Although it might not cost lives as in Lord Raglan's day, your next communication error could result in a lost contract or client, or even a damaged personal relationship.

THREE KEYS TO ACTIVE LISTENING

To avoid these communication errors, I will share with you the three keys to active listening:

#1. effectively preparing for conversations
#2. being mindfully present as conversations take place
#3. asking the right questions to clarify and avoid miscommunication

I hope you will take away the active listening techniques I will describe that make up these three steps, to allow you to avoid dangerous errors of communication. With these three keys, you can become an active listener with more successful relationships.

As an experienced relationship coach, I spend several hours most days listening to real people as they outline their difficult situations. I have helped many people through uncertain and difficult times, and my goal has always been servant leadership to meet their deepest needs. Often times when I find myself working with men in divorce situations or couples in troubled relationships, my chief goal is to help them communicate more effectively. I constantly find poor communication at the root of relationship difficulties, and often observe how even modest improvements in communication can have transformative impacts.

Especially while working with men facing divorce, the most dramatic breakthroughs have been observable in small group situations, where communication channels were open and the environment was accepting. Even simply practicing this first step, to 'seek first to understand', has helped many see what they have been missing and take the initial step to commit to listening actively. Once they share their breakthrough, these men feel a sense of accomplishment and take the next steps. Their journey to learn how to actively listen encourages each of us as they share their personal victories with the group.

KEY #1: BE PREPARED TO LISTEN ACTIVELY

Active listening is, to begin with, a mindset. As Dr. Steven Covey notes, the most important relationship principle is to 'Seek first to understand, then to be understood.'

Keep an open mind: defer judgements & avoid assumptions

If you're like most people, you probably seek first to be understood; you want to get your point across. And in so doing, your unintended consequences may include ignoring the other person completely, conveying that you are only pretending to listen, or selectively hearing only certain parts of the conversation to focus only on the words being said, missing the intended meaning entirely.

So why does this happen? Simply put, because most people listen with the intent to reply, not to understand. You begin to prepare in your mind what you are going to say, the questions you are going to ask, etc. You filter everything you hear through your life experiences, through your own individual frame of reference. You check what you hear against your autobiography and see how it measures up. And consequently, you decide prematurely what the other person means before he or she finishes speaking. Does any of this sound familiar?

Know your audience

Know your audience by listening carefully and completely. Do not rush to judgement but allow all information to be considered. If you have a prior relationship with the speaker, think about how you can build trust and show integrity by giving the other person your attention in the way they prefer.

Putting your focus on the other person in your conversation will create important shifts in your thinking that will positively benefit your relationship. As Warren Buffet has noted, "Even modest improvements in your communication skills can provide a tremendous benefit in the long term."

KEY #2: GIVE FOCUSED ATTENTION ON THE CONVERSATION – BE MINDFULLY PRESENT

It may surprise you to hear that great oratory skills may not be required for you to be a great communicator. Although public speaking is a valuable asset, putting together a message that can be delivered effectively is often only achievable through careful listening and consideration of others' points of view.

By successfully employing your active listening skills, you can learn to effectively incorporate the feedback of your colleagues, employees, and family members to improve outcomes both at home and in your professional life. Once you have completed your initial preparation as an active listener by keeping an open mind and thinking carefully about your audience, it's time to employ the next key: give focused attention on the conversation – be mindfully present.

Body language signals your interest and engagement with the speaker

To be mindfully present is to shut out the outside world as much as possible, while focusing completely on the speaker. Your attention will be reflected in the physical signals you are sending to the speaker.

Adjusting your body language can strengthen your communications and help you make a better impression in all kinds of social and professional settings. Facial expressions, hand gestures, and posture all communicate certain meanings. When considering the body language required for active listening, remember that the main idea is to physically show you are actively engaging with the speaker.

- Make eye contact. While there may be cultural differences, subtle eye contact is often interpreted as being friendly and honest. Look people in the eye when first introduced. As someone is talking, meet their eye from time to time to show interest, but avoid staring.
- Hold your head up. Keep your head raised to appear more confident and approachable.
- Smile and nod judiciously. Nod your head slightly to let someone know they have your attention, and you are listening intently to what they are saying. Your smiling face is your best asset and helps put others at ease.

The key to these non-verbal cues is that we are active and engaged, and our audience is important to us. Remember to treat non-verbal communication holistically, as we can all give off unintended signals that tend to lack congruence with our message.

We should also note that personal confidence is a huge component of body language. Lacking sufficient confidence, you may be impatient if the person you are speaking with initially struggles to make their point clearly. Try not to react but rather seek to show patience and continue to listen without judgment. This will give the speaker the chance to clarify and make themself understood.

Don't interrupt!

It is a grammar school truism that silence is golden. As Will Rogers once noted in his own colorful style: "Never miss a good chance to shut up." Our silence conveys respect to the speaker and their message.

Be receptive to how the other person is feeling

When you initially meet someone, your body language will speak volumes without saying a word, so be mindful of the initial signals you send. In one-on-one communication, my best recommendation is to build trust by developing rapport with that person via mirroring.

Pay close attention to their posture, their speech pattern, their energy level and any major non-verbal cue they may exhibit. In simplest terms, you mirror that individual. If they speak softly, you lower your voice. If they speak quickly, you will follow their lead.

Mirroring is a proven technique to break down initial human barriers in a wide variety of situations. As you follow the body language cues above, do not neglect to learn and develop the art of mirroring to see how much smoother your conversations can become. Try it out with someone in your life that can be a bit difficult, to see if you arrive at a different outcome.

KEY #3: ASK QUESTIONS TO CLARIFY AND UNDERSTAND

When we seek first to understand, doesn't communication become a process? When an active listener receives the initial message, we probably need more information to understand. We begin to clarify that message by asking questions to answer unknowns. We soon learn that open-ended questions give us our best answers.

Reflect back – restate and paraphrase

Next, we reflect and paraphrase or restate our understanding. We can continue to ask our next open-ended questions until we feel we have our questions answered. The interaction with the speaker is often brief, but our process to internally parse this communication continues. Learning to ask better questions is a powerful tool to become a more gifted communicator and to truly understand.

Defer judgments, whether agreement or disagreement

Don't make assumptions. Wait until the speaker is finished before formulating opinions. Strong emotions often cloud communications, and we must keep an open mind through the process to understand the message. It's hard not to think about what you are going to say next when there is disagreement, but we must resist the temptation to shut down thought when we get what we want, or when we disagree.

Whether we agree or disagree with the message, we can't allow these emotions to interrupt our intentions to understand the speaker. Active listening calls for strong emotional intelligence to hear the message and further clarify while seeking to finally understand. We must not formulate opinions before we have enough information. Don't stop processing before you understand the message, simply because strong emotions have been triggered.

Listen to understand, not to respond

As Peter Drucker notes, "The most important thing in communication is hearing what isn't said."

When you are strong emotionally and actively process communications until you understand, then you have become an exceptional communicator.

The next target is to learn and develop the skill of hearing what was not said. Complex communication always carries elements of ambiguity. Once the speaker has finished delivering their message, learn to train your inner dialogue to paint the complete picture by looking to understand what was not said.

CONCLUSION

In our initial story outlining the senseless tragedy of *The Charge of the Light Brigade*, we see how multiple occurrences of all three major communication errors led to great tragedy.

1. Errors of Transmission
2. Errors of Reception
3. Errors of Context, or Perspective

Active listening could have stopped this tragic tale at multiple points prior to tragedy. You too can avoid these errors in future. Active listening helps provide more complete information. With more complete information, you can make better decisions.

Active listening is a process and begins with a mindset. Our goal is to listen to understand. Learn to listen with an open mind, and defer judgements as you pull in the information. Avoid assumptions as you listen. Remember to listen not to respond, but instead to understand. Know your audience and maintain good body posture to assure the speaker that you are fully engaged. Always try to defer judgement while you listen.

As the speaker wraps up, process the information you have received. Gather additional information by asking open-ended questions to paint the complete picture. Continue the process of asking questions until you feel you have sufficient information. Be emotionally mature, and patiently defer judgement as you pull in the information. Finally, reflect on all you know.

With all the information you have received, ask yourself if the essential data is complete or at least more complete. You should now arrive at a place where you more fully understand the speaker. With more and better information, do you feel more confident in making better decisions?

Congratulations! You now know the techniques to avoid the three major communication errors. These active listening techniques will enable you to listen to understand. Successful application of the techniques presented in this chapter will provide the foundation to push for better understanding in all your communications. Continue to exercise these techniques and you will become an excellent communicator with better relationships.

About Clifton

Clifton Holden (AKA MyCoach Clifton) shepherds his clients through some of their most difficult days as a relationship coach. Clients often arrive contemplating divorce or even have begun proceedings. Many only agree to counseling as a last resort. He works with clients to the relationship to which they are committed.

Clifton is a graduate of McMurry University in Abilene, Texas. Following a career in IT and oilfield services with IBM, Halliburton and other IBM business partners, he began his transition into coaching. In 2019, he received his initial formal training from Strategic Intervention which is now associated with Robbins-Madanes Training. World events in early 2020 provide the perfect time and place to work full time as a relationship coach and he fully embraces his opportunity.

Clifton meets clients both in 1:1 and in group coaching settings. His group coaching for men in wobbly relationships and divorce provides a safe place for men to positively handle the stages of divorce. Research proves how difficult the process of divorce is for men and his groups fill multiple critical needs as his guys step through the divorce process. He also works to meet the growing need among his male clients in the midst of gray divorce.

Clifton finds mission and ministry in the opportunities given to work with his clients. He remains committed to finding the best for his clients in their every situation.

You can contact Clifton at:
- clifton@mycoachclifton.com
- www.facebook.com/mycoachcclifton
- www.instagram.com/mycoachclifton

CHAPTER 5

THE FIVE PILLARS OF LEVERAGE

BY JUSTIN WALLNER

"I just don't get it," the young protégé lamented. "I've been coming here at dawn every day for three years helping you plant these seeds. The plants have not grown at all. Countless times we've walked up and down the side of this river planting and watering. When are we going to see some results?"

The old wise man looked up the river at the horizon, wiping sweat from his brow. "Patience, young man. We do this for good reason and its part of your training. Three years ago, you came to me so eager to learn my secrets to become as wise and wealthy as I am. Have you forgotten?" he asked.

"Of course not. But when are we going to see progress? I want to start making money."

The old man smiled back at him and replied, "Patience..."

THE FIVE PILLARS

You can leverage earth, air, fire, water and metal. You can leverage your money, minutes, mind, muscles and motivation, or that of other people (OPM). You can leverage your social circle – your family, friends, colleagues, mentors and network. But nothing is as powerful as the committed, determined and resilient desire of an indestructible will rising forth from deep within your soul. Deep down within you, buried below all your excuses, fears, failures, limiting beliefs and negative influences, is a dormant volcano of potential that is an absolute force of nature. When you summon your most magnificent inner power, you can achieve almost *anything.*

PILLAR I: COMMIT TO EXCELLENCE

I'm truly honored to co-author this book on *Leverage* with world-renowned business legend Brian Tracy, an Apex Leader who has sold millions of copies of his books and trained millions of leaders in every aspect of business. As a master of Time Leverage, he teaches leadership, sales, personal development, time management, writing, speaking, goal setting and monetization.

Recently, I also co-authored *Success* with Jack Canfield, an Apex Leader who overcame rejection from 144 publishers to create the *Chicken Soup for the Soul* series. In it, I wrote that *Eudaimonia* (Aristotle's concept of happiness) is a lifelong pursuit of success in five areas – Health, Wealth, Friendship, Knowledge and Virtue. Applying this to leverage, we have Physical Leverage, Financial Leverage, Social Leverage, Mental Leverage and Spiritual Leverage.

Growing up, I endured great adversity. Humble beginnings in a rough neighborhood brought with it challenges of many kinds to overcome. Rather than identify as a victim, I decided to be victorious by not allowing life to break me. I knew God was on my side to protect and deliver me from harm, making me fearless and unbreakable. Just as extreme pressure transforms coal into diamonds, adversity made me strong. This is the power of Spiritual Leverage. It steels our resolve, giving us strength or Emotional Leverage to fuel our will to persevere in conquering fear and trials.

Emotional Leverage helped me to survive and thrive. It gave me courage and made me tough through seven years of football and the rest of my career. With time and conditioning, courage was transformed to Physical Leverage on the football field. I added fuel to the fire with daily success habits like running five miles and pumping iron for hours.

Motivated to become more effective in sports and self-defense, I took massive action and made exponential progress. Within six months, I increased my bench press from 35 to 185 lbs, which inspired my *big audacious goal* of winning a weightlifting competition. Within a few years, I had bench pressed 315 lbs., deadlifted 500 lbs., leg pressed 1,000 lbs., and won a weightlifting competition. I say that not to impress you, but rather to impress upon you what is possible with hard work, discipline and commitment to worthy goals.

Physical Leverage bought me Social Leverage as it earned the respect of my peers. This trend continued after my transition from California to Oregon. While visiting my father for the summer, I started lifting weights at the local High School and was invited by their head coach to join the football team. So, I did, with the blessing of my mother and father. When I was just about to give up, years of prayers were answered with a new lease on life.

Commitment to excellence *must* bring you success over time. Provided you don't quit on your goals, you *will* succeed! You will also inspire others to follow suit. We call this "leadership by example." Furthermore, by mastering your daily success habits in each area of leverage, you will align your energetic frequency with some of the most successful people in the world. The better your daily habits are, the more positive your energy is, the more powerful and well-defined your goals are, the stronger your will is, and the more you grow as a person the higher your frequency will be. This will attract people who are also on a higher frequency. We attract what we are.

PILLAR II: FIND A NEED AND FILL IT

When I was seven years old, I experienced a radical paradigm shift that shaped my thinking and served me well in life and business. It started when my brother and I decided it was time to earn some extra money. My brother instigated this pivotal mastermind and business brainstorming session. I remember him asking how we might be able to make some extra money. Our financial education began as we gazed out our upstairs bedroom window.

As I stared at the horizon above our local golf course, suddenly it hit me. We were sitting on a gold mine. I remembered walking our dog Princess on the golf course and the many stray golf balls we would find there and in our back yard. With so many golfers losing their golf balls, there was clearly a need for them. This was Commerce 101 – they had the *demand*, and we had the *supply*.

"Let's sell golf balls to golfers!" I exclaimed. Just like that, our first business venture was born. "What else can we sell to them?" Two things were clear to us: they all needed golf balls and they all needed a drink. Much to their dismay, we were too young to sell beer. But we could sell sodas and water all day long. They were always on sale at the store and free golf balls were easy to clean. Our parents gave us their blessing, support, and some seed capital (OPM) to help us help ourselves.

We did well for a couple of boys on the hunt and learned invaluable lessons about sales, communication, customer service, marketing and business. Incidentally, most of my success in life has been achieved in these areas. For the first time in our young lives, we learned to transform our Physical and Mental Leverage into Financial Leverage. Our business enjoyed generous margins and profits remained lucrative for several summers of cold hard cash.

PILLAR III: ALWAYS ADD VALUE

If you want to achieve greatness, you must begin by leveraging the knowledge, wisdom and success secrets of those who have successfully attained that which you desire. This will allow you to gain leverage over your Thoughts, Beliefs and Habits. Once you have established a firm grasp of your own self-mastery, the next step on your road to success is to leverage the best of your abilities to acquire "high income skills" that will allow you to add value to the marketplace. With your newfound skills and abilities, you must then deliver the greatest amount of value that you possibly can. After all, you cannot achieve and maintain great wealth without delivering great value.

During pre-season conditioning in Oregon, I strained my Achilles tendons, pulled both hamstrings and broke my finger. My first days at school were spent hobbling around campus on crutches. After school, I got my ankles wrapped and went to practice every day. As a lineman, I played every down of every game that season – offense, defense, and special teams.

Despite all this adversity, I was immensely grateful to have a second chance at life in a town with great people. My *big audacious goal* was now to achieve my highest potential. I got to work on my grades and immersed myself in school to make up for lost time. My alarm clock was set to "Eye of the Tiger" and sounded off at 5:00 am every morning.

In five years, I won fifty awards including a Congressional Nomination to the Air Force Academy. Though I was unable to attend due to injuries, this paid huge dividends in Social Capital. I was also selected to represent my state at Presidential Classroom, a leadership forum in Washington, D.C. There I gained tremendous Social Leverage, meeting Senators on Capitol Hill and working with a retired Lieutenant Colonel who was then the Mission Director of Air Force One and Senior Aide to then President George W. Bush. We led a project together with a team of sixty researching post-9/11 security policy, the findings of which I presented at Georgetown University.

When injuries ended my football career, I invested heavily in Mental Capital by joining the Speech and Debate team. I won many awards in tournaments and continued in college, adding great value to our teams. I volunteered with Phi Theta Kappa Honor Society, a scholastic and service organization. As VP of Service, I led our chapter in creating "Date Auction Concoction" – a major charity event with dozens of sponsors that raised thousands of dollars for American Cancer Society. We were featured live-in-studio on ABC morning news.

When I campaigned for International VP at the annual convention, the Executive Director interviewed me live on film at Anaheim Hilton Hotel, which broadcasted it on their TV network and at nearby hotels for several days. Forty-five chapters voted for me, but not quite enough to win. Elected instead as Regional Vice President, I advised twenty-five College Deans and Chapters about charity-event planning, public relations and marketing. In 2004, Hawaii Pacific University recruited me on a Phi Theta Kappa scholarship for Leadership and Service.

PILLAR IV: ALIGN WITH WINNERS

Andrew Carnegie, founder of Carnegie Steel, was one of the wealthiest men to ever live, even though he arrived in America as a poor Scottish immigrant with almost no money. He gave most of his fortune away in grants, scholarships, endowments, Carnegie Hall, Carnegie Library, etc. Having spent his life aligning with winners and always adding value, he became exceedingly wealthy and brought into his network the most influential titans of industry in all fields. He acquired great wealth and influence by surrounding himself with high performance people. He attracted them because he was like them.

He leveraged the magnificent author Napoleon Hill, who worked without pay for twenty years on his greatest legacy project. He had Napoleon interview the wealthiest people in the world and share their secrets in a guidebook for riches and prosperity. That book is *Think and Grow Rich*, one of the top bestselling books of all time. What made Andrew Carnegie so wealthy? He caught a trend early and became the master of steel, the hottest commodity of the day.

Your network is your net worth, and you attract who you are. All you must do to attract titans of industry is become one. If you want to attract influential mentors and friends, you must get on their frequency. The easiest way to do so is to adopt the mindset and daily habits of successful people and make them permanent. Until you can leverage working relationships with Apex Leaders, you must leverage their books and the content they provide. For example, Brian Tracy helped me overcome procrastination through his bestselling book, *Eat That Frog*. I benefit greatly from his books and countless hours of his content.

The richest people build networks. In 2008, while living in Hawaii, a mentor gave me *The 21 Irrefutable Laws of Leadership*, by John C. Maxwell, another Apex Leader whom I later met. It inspired a *big audacious goal* to work directly with the world's most influential leaders. We become the five people we spend the most time with, so I made friends with CEO's, billionaires, philanthropists, the founder of a major cell phone provider and a retired Wall Street executive.

In 2009, a friend recruited me as Marketing Director for his talent management company in Los Angeles. After expanding my network there, I became the Chief Marketing Officer of Miss Asia USA and helped to plan pageants. I then began planning networking events in Beverly Hills and Ascent Expo at LA Convention Center, where the founder of World Film Institute recruited me as his publicist. After adding great value in marketing, promotions and event planning, he promoted me to the position of Vice President. Years later, I co-produced the

21st Anniversary Family Film Awards Celebration event with Oscar, Emmy, and Golden Globe Winners. I also served on the Host Committee of CITY Gala & Summit, planning philanthropic events with celebrities.

PILLAR V: BUILD APEX LEVERAGE
(SELF-ACTUALIZATION VIBRATION)

Apex Leaders positively impact the lives of millions of people, leaving a powerful legacy of influence that goes on for decades, centuries or even millennia. They lead from a place of self-actualization, the pinnacle of Maslow's Pyramid or Hierarchy of Needs. The base of this five-level pyramid represents our basic "physiological needs" for food, water, warmth, rest, etc. Once these needs are met, we move up to our "safety needs" for security and protection, followed by our "belongingness and love needs", and then our "esteem needs" relating to respect. At the top of the pyramid, we reach the peak of "self-actualization" or living our full potential.

What is the secret of Apex Leaders? They set *big audacious goals* that bring out the best in others, helping them to achieve their highest potential. They pull people at every level into self-actualization, inspiring them to rise with a compelling vision or True North Star. In *Success*, I wrote about finding your own. If you want to use leverage to make a fortune, find a way to meet the needs of the many at any level. If you want to create Apex Leverage or Legacy Wealth, focus on meeting the self-actualization needs of others.

During the Cold War, the Soviets were leading in the 'Space Race' until President John F. Kennedy declared a *big audacious goal* that we would be the first nation to land a man on the moon within a decade. This ignited an "all-hands-on-deck" effort in the sciences, landed a man on the moon and helped us win the Cold War. Jesus Christ proclaimed a *big audacious goal* to make disciples of all nations. His message inspired America's founders and still endures 2,000 years later, partly thanks to people like Reverend Dr. Martin Luther King, Jr. who powerfully stated the *big audacious goal* of racial equality in America: "I have a dream that my four little children will one day live in a nation where they will not be judged by the color of their skin, but by their character."

The late legend and Apex Leader, Detective Frank Shankwitz, may he rest in peace, is one of the greatest men I have ever known. He was the Creator and Co-Founder of Make-A-Wish Foundation, an organization that has granted the wishes of over 500,000 children around the world, many of whom don't have long to live. I am honored to have called him my friend. He gave several keynote addresses at our business networking events in Beverly Hills where I spent time with him, sometimes as his driver. His legacy will carry on forever through the millions of families he helped. Make-A-Wish is a great cause to support, and I am always recommending *Wish Man*, the movie based on his life story and the beginning of this wonderful organization.

SEEDS OF WISDOM

... The young man walked through the forest.

After five long years, he was growing to resent the process. What wisdom could the old man possibly impart? It was time to move on. He raised his head up for one last look. Minutes passed as he stood there quietly, staring down the river, shocked in disbelief. As far as the eye could see, dotting the riverbank in majestic harmony, were hundreds of three-foot-tall bamboo stalks lined up in a row. He was stunned.

"Now do you understand?" said the old wise man as he emerged from the forest. "We've been planting bamboo trees all these years. It takes time for the roots to grow underground. When the tree finally breaks ground, it grows fast – sometimes three

feet per day. These trees grow sixty to ninety feet tall, often in sixty to ninety days. Keep watering. Now that we have momentum, we must never let it die.

"This forest is a metaphor for life. You must keep to your daily disciplines for many moons to see visible results, which will become exponential over time. Soon we will have a robust bamboo forest. Bamboo is resilient and has many uses, strong as steel yet durable and pliable. It can be used to build houses and furniture worth good money. Other trees crack and break in strong wind, bamboo merely bends with it.

"You, young man, are like bamboo. By practicing daily discipline with good habits, you are leveraging time itself and growing just as fast. But daily discipline with bad habits is like a slow burning ember that burns it all to ash.

"Always guard your forest. Invest in seeds and workers, with your own money if you must. Better to leverage other people's money from grants, loans, or selling small shares of future harvesting. Reinvest profits to grow the business with compound interest. Avoid buying luxuries until much harvesting buys them for you. Pay your lenders promptly until much harvesting makes you a lender earning interest.

"One day, with the right plan in place to harvest, reshape, and distribute the bamboo, you will provide many jobs and make our town very prosperous. In time, you will be the wisest and wealthiest man in the land."

About Justin

Justin Wallner is a Best-Selling Author, Business Consultant and Master Marketer who empowers worthy entrepreneurs with higher levels of Success.

In 2020, Mr. Wallner joined forces with *Chicken Soup for the Soul* creator Jack Canfield to co-author the bestselling book, *SUCCESS: The World's Leading Entrepreneurs and Professionals Reveal Their Success Secrets to Help You Live a Happier, Healthier, and Wealthier Life.*

At age 17, he met with Senators on Capitol Hill, received a Congressional Nomination to the Air Force Academy, and spoke at Georgetown University. He was welcomed to the stage by a former Lieutenant Colonel serving as Air Force One Mission Director for then-President George W. Bush. Together, they led a research team that recommended security policies adding to the discussion of the Homeland Security Act of 2002. Mr. Wallner presented the findings to hundreds of leaders, Congresspeople and one of the President's Cabinet Members.

As Regional Vice President of Phi Theta Kappa Honor Society, he advised twenty-five College Deans and student leaders in marketing, public relations and fundraising for American Cancer Society events. He and his team were featured "live in studio" on ABC Channel 2 Morning News in 2003.

Mr. Wallner has been seen in *Forbes, Yahoo News, Huffington Post, LA Times,* etc. He has worked as Vice President of World Film Institute, Chief Marketing Officer of Miss Asia USA, and Marketing Director for World Financial Group, raising millions of dollars for his clients.

He planned business networking events in Beverly Hills with Higher Xperience, guest speakers including Napoleon Hill Foundation authors Sharon Lechter and Dr. Greg Reid, founder of Secret Knock, as well as late legends Frank Shankwitz, founder of Make-A-Wish Foundation, Olympic Silver Medalist Steve Jennings, CITY Gala founder Ryan Long and CEO Space founder Berny Dohrmann, who interviewed Justin in 2013.

Mr. Wallner co-produced the 21st Anniversary Family Film Awards Celebration

Event with Oscar, Emmy and Golden Globe Winners. He helped to revive World Film Institute twenty years after it joined Dick Clark Productions for the Family Film Awards on CBS in 1996. The show's Executive Producer was late legend Dick Clark, who joined Charlton Heston in presenting awards to Bob Hope, Ron Howard, Tom Hanks, Sandra Bullock, Neve Campbell, etc.

As a Member of the CITY Gala & Summit Host Committee, he helped to facilitate charity events with celebrity guest speakers including Jack Canfield, Astronaut Buzz Aldrin, Sir Richard Branson, John Paul DeJoria, Matthew McConaughey, John Travolta, Halle Berry, Ashton Kutcher, Tai Lopez, etc.

For more information on how to grow your business, contact Mr. Wallner on social media or his website at:

- http://www.JustinWallner.com

CHAPTER 6

THE BUSINESS TRIFECTA: THE SECRET FORMULA FOR MEDIA SUCCESS

BY NICK NANTON & JW DICKS

Success is simple. Do what's right, the right way, at the right time.
~ Arnold H. Glasgow

Imagine a new movie studio starting up with modest means. Anxious to get off on the right foot, they put every dollar into making the most amazing feature film anyone has ever seen.

Note two critical words in that last sentence: "every dollar." Because when the studio finishes this amazing movie, they have no money left to market it. They can't get anyone to see it because they don't have any funds to tell anyone about it.

Anxious not to repeat that mistake, they raise more money and put a bundle into hiring the best movie marketing company in the country to sell their next very-modestly budgeted film. The marketing company delivers to them an amazing film trailer and TV commercials.

Except, again, they've spent everything. Now they have no

71

money to do the PR (Public Relations) to do the all-important press junket and get the stars on the late-night talk shows.

The moral of this story? You can't properly grow your company without the right 'business trifecta'—the perfect combination of media, marketing and PR. Over-emphasizing one over the other leads to an imbalance, just as if you tried to sit on a stool with two legs.

First let's walk through all three of the elements we're talking about here, so you can better understand why each is important. We'll start with...

MEDIA

Entrepreneurs and professionals create media to sell an aspect of their businesses—it could simply be an image-booster, useful information or more of a hard-sell pitch. Media can be in the form of a brochure, a video, an audio CD, a book, etc.

This kind of media is usually not a client's main business, even though media can be sold just like any informational product. For instance, a tax specialist could write a book on tax secrets. That book could then be sold on Amazon, even though the specialist's main business is, obviously, helping his or her own clients with their tax issues. The book serves as an indirect advertisement for the specialist.

Of course, it's sometimes more worthwhile to give the media away for free to generate leads, establish expertise and grab contact info for future marketing. Downloadable information on company websites that require an email entry for access to that kind of media is a prime example of that.

When producing media, it's really important to look at your target market and your distribution method, to make sure that your media is produced in a fashion that will be in-line with the distribution method and target audience. Note here we're not saying that it all has to look like it came out of a Hollywood studio, because, even with a Hollywood studio, sometimes you want it to look "home brewed" (think *The Blair Witch Project*).

Whatever your creative approach, the presentation of the media and the packaging can be the first step in establishing the critical elements of credibility and trust. But again, no matter how good your media is, you still need...

MARKETING

How do you let your target group and/or customer base know that your media, which is probably of great interest to them, is out there and available? Well, that's where marketing comes into play.

Marketing can involve everything from low-cost viral videos to highly-polished TV spots, from free emails to expensive direct mail campaigns, from simple robo-calls to sophisticated referral programs. Marketing is how you get prospects to either buy what you're selling or, at the very least, get them to take a good look at you.

The purpose of your marketing, of course, can be multi-faceted. You may want to drive people to your website...and then, have your website convince them to leave their contact info...and then generate an email sequence designed to get them to buy. Or you may want a simple, targeted campaign with just one end result in mind—a simple sales letter designed to get people to buy your product, for example.

But either way, once you've done that, it's time to employ...

PR - PUBLIC RELATIONS

PR, or Public Relations, is all about creating awareness. You know the age-old question: if a tree falls in a forest and nobody's around, does it make a sound? Well, PR doesn't really care about the answer to that question—it just wants to make sure somebody is around to hear when that tree hits the ground.

That awareness comes primarily from press releases and media appearances. When your business has sold its one millionth widget (or whatever it is you sell), that's impressive to people—so you want them to know about it, because it boosts the image of your company. That's why you want to put out a special press release about that special widget, both online and offline.

If that press release hits at the right time, it could land you a story in the newspaper, in a magazine, on the radio, TV or online. It can also get you invited on radio and TV interview shows to talk about that special millionth widget. Or, if it's an online press release, it could just drive more traffic to your website—which, if you've got your ducks in a row, could end up being far more profitable than any media appearance you could get!

(By the way, that's why we mostly concentrate on the online press release, rather than the old-school offline variety. Online press releases boost your internet presence and, since they're written in the third person, also act as powerful online testimonials to anyone Googling you or your business – and its ROI is pretty much guaranteed.)

Should you nab those special media appearances, stories, and the traffic to your website, the great thing is you got it all *totally free.* Your main cost might come from hiring a PR company to help you make all of that happen. But, unless you have a legitimate story that really does stand out, that PR firm might be hard-pressed to get you much of an afterlife beyond that initial press release.

As a matter of fact, that's one of the biggest mistakes we see companies make—hiring PR firms when they don't have the marketing or media to back it up. When you try to get PR and you don't really have a story to tell…well, let's get back to that tree-falling-in-the-forest fable. In this case, there are people around to hear it—but nobody really bothers to listen.
Which is why we came up with….

THE SECRET FORMULA

How you put all three of these elements together—media, marketing and PR—is critically important. If you don't allocate enough money and resources to each one of them, and/or if you don't use each of them in the right way—you'll end up spending a lot of money without much to show for your efforts.

What we'd like to do is walk you through our "secret formula" for using all three in an orchestrated and effective system for our CelebrityPress™ authors. We're not doing this to toot our own horn, but, quite honestly, it's one of the few all-in-one campaigns that we know of.

First of all, as we noted before, we produce a great high-quality hardcover book that's got an attractive eye-catching cover, powerful overall theme and the participation of great authors. Those authors usually only have to worry about contributing a chapter rather than generating an entire book—making it much easier on their end. They still get credit for authoring the book, however, and can order special customized copies of the book with their picture on the cover. That takes care of the **media** portion of the program—because our client now has a terrific product around which he or she can build the marketing and PR.

Next, comes the **marketing**. We've created a targeted marketing

75

system that guarantees each one of our books becomes a best-seller on Amazon. The other half of that marketing formula is that we give our authors over thirty ways to use their new best-seller to market their business. Having a book is a great attention-getter, but having a *best-selling book* is impressive on a whole different level. So, again, we're handling the marketing to make the book a Best Seller, which will get it lots of attention, and at the same time, our authors are using more than thirty of our marketing strategies simultaneously to market the book to their own audiences to create a far greater impact.

And that carries over to the **PR**. Remember when we said you needed to have a real story to tell when you put out press releases (another way to think about it is "you've got to *find* the news in what you're doing)? Well, a best-selling book gives you that story. Our PR starts by putting out a press release that says so-and-so has signed a publishing deal with CelebrityPress™, and then, after publication, the all-important follow-up press release that proclaims our author's book has achieved best-selling status. Those press releases spur media outlets to pursue any one of our authors for stories and interviews about their new book and, of course, their business.

Everything feeds into each other—but all of it springs from the fact that we have created a *real* media product as well as a *real* story about that media product. Which brings us to the magic ingredient of our special formula…

MELDING MEDIA

What we left out of our discussion of media earlier in this chapter is the fact that there are *two kinds of media.*

Mass media is the type most people know about. We're talking about commercial TV networks, national magazines, radio stations, etc. that are operated specifically to bring in consumers of all stripes. Mass media is about numbers—they want to attract the most users, so they can't really mess around; they must produce content that's genuine and interesting to the most people or they lose money.

All of us put the "mass" into mass media—we seek it out every day by watching our favorite shows, reading our favorite newspapers, listening to our favorite music and so forth. And because it has no other visible agenda than to entertain and inform the most people, mass media automatically brings two things to the table—awareness and credibility. If there's a story about you on CNN, people (1) see it, and (2) think more of you because of it (unless, of course, you just murdered somebody or something...but we won't get into that here!).

This is why people hire PR companies – to get them on mass media outlets. The problem is, you cannot "eat" awareness and credibility—in other words, if there isn't a direct solicitation involved with a mass media appearance, it's not really a big revenue generator. You're a story for a day and then it disappears (another reason we prefer online PR—it pretty much stays online forever!).

Now, let's talk about the second kind of media, known as "direct media." This is more of a targeted informational sales tool that takes the form of a CD, DVD, newsletter, direct mail piece, website copy, etc. The business distributes this direct media to an audience it selects (or in most cases the audience has identified itself by "opting in" on the website), with the sole purpose of selling to that audience—and it's created by that business for that specific purpose.

The problem? *Direct media lacks credibility.* There's a reason direct mail campaigns only have an average response rate of between 2 and 3 percent. Whenever anyone knows that a business is directly trying to sell to them, they immediately put up their guard and get suspicious. They don't know if what the sales piece is telling them is true because they know that the company is mainly interested in their money.

One way around this credibility gap is to use testimonials and product reviews, and other third-party verification that appears objective. But there's still another way around it that takes the cake...

...and that's melding *both* kinds of media—mass media and direct media—into one.

For example, when you talk about having a best-selling book (mass media) in your direct media, that gives you an awesome level of

credibility you wouldn't otherwise have. We also often place our clients on shows that appear on NBC, CBS, ABC, FOX and other national outlets. They can then talk about those mass media appearances in their direct media. If someone sees those network logos on your direct mail piece or your website, again, you're suddenly elevated in their eyes to a national expert (which you may already be—but would have a hard time convincing a stranger of that fact otherwise).

But any business person can do the same thing. For example, you use PR to get on mass media—television, radio, newspapers/magazines—the fastest and easiest way you possibly can. Then you take your direct media, stuff you can easily control the cost and distribution of, and put your mass media credibility in the direct media.

In other words, say you managed to get a spot on CNBC talking about your business. You trumpet that fact on your website, your newsletter, your e-zine, whatever direct media piece you create. That mass media "stamp of approval" can mean the world to a potential customer and can mean the difference between them paying attention instead of throwing it in the trash—and we all know the ROI on the trash can!

Even better is if you post a copy of that mass media appearance on your website, or put a copy of your newspaper article into a direct mail piece. We even hang ours up on our office walls—and our clients will invariably comment on them, which inevitably leads to us telling those clients how they can get the same coverage for themselves.

So, ask yourself – don't you think that kind of mass media "stamp of approval" will get you taken a little bit more seriously? We can tell you, based on literally hundreds of case studies, it absolutely will get people to pay closer attention to you and what you have to offer.

So, get yourself some mass media credibility—and insert it into your direct media. Don't spend all your time and money trying to get on TV or in the paper without having a plan for using that mass media exposure—in conjunction with direct media for your marketing.

When you successfully combine media, marketing and PR, you're guaranteed business growth and increased revenues. Correctly leveraging the business trifecta raises your enterprise to the next level—and trust us, you will enjoy the view from up there!

About Nick

From the slums of Port au Prince, Haiti with special forces raiding a sex trafficking ring and freeing children; to the Virgin Galactic Space Port in Mojave with Sir Richard Branson, Nick is passionate about telling stories that connect.

He has directed more than 60 documentaries and a sold-out Broadway Show (garnering 43 Emmy nominations in multiple regional and national competitions, and 22 wins). He has made films and shows featuring: Larry King, Jack Nicklaus, Tony Robbins, Sir Richard Branson, Dean Kamen, Lisa Nichols, Peter Diamandis and many more. He is currently the host of *In Case You Didn't Know…with Nick Nanton* on Amazon Prime, and regularly hosts the podcast Now to Next with Nick Nanton which can be found on all popular podcast platforms.

Nick also enjoys serving as an Elder at Orangewood Church, supporting Young Life, Entrepreneurs International and rooting for the Florida Gators with his wife Kristina and their three children, Brock, Bowen and Addison.

Learn more at:
- www.NickNanton.com
- www.CelebrityBrandingAgency.com
- www.DNAmedia.com

About JW

JW Dicks, Esq., is the CEO of DN Agency, an Inc. 5000 Multimedia Company that represents over 3,000 clients in 63 countries.

He is a *Wall Street Journal* Best-Selling Author® who has authored or co-authored over 47 books, a 7-time Emmy® Award-winning Executive Producer and a Broadway Show Producer.

JW is an Ansari XPRIZE Innovation Board member, Chairman of the Board of the National Retirement Council™, Chairman of the Board of the National Academy of Best-Selling Authors®, Board Member of the National Association of Experts, Writers and Speakers®, and a Board Member of the International Academy of Film Makers®.

He has been quoted on business and financial topics in national media such as *USA Today, The Wall Street Journal, Newsweek, Forbes, CNBC.com,* and *Fortune Magazine Small Business.*

JW has co-authored books with legends like Jack Canfield, Brian Tracy, Tom Hopkins, Dr. Nido Qubein, Steve Forbes, Richard Branson, Michael Gerber, Dr. Ivan Misner, and Dan Kennedy.

JW has appeared and interviewed on business television shows airing on ABC, NBC, CBS, and FOX affiliates around the country and co-produces and syndicates a line of franchised business television shows such as *Success Today, Wall Street Today, Hollywood Live,* and *Profiles of Success.*

JW and his wife of 47 years, Linda, have two daughters, and four granddaughters. He is a sixth-generation Floridian and splits his time between his home in Orlando and his beach house on Florida's west coast.

CHAPTER 7

LISTEN TO 'SILENCE'
...TO HEAR THE CELEBRATION BEHIND THE GALAXIES!

BY ANAHIT ETEMADI

Once upon a time, I was a conglomeration of energies bouncing harmoniously in a dark space, somewhere in a faraway galaxy... one of 125 billion! I was happy with my existence...dancing with my innate motion...an organized choreography...chanting the magical "Word"!

My gift was the ability to evolve to different levels of vibrations, without seeing, smelling, hearing, touching or any other sense. In the solid, dark silence, while communicating intelligently and harmoniously with other energies around me... we were "one," happily dancing and chanting the "Word".

At one point, a group of energies that were passing by, sent me a telepathic message: "There are other beautiful and magical worlds...with lights, colors and objects. You will soon reach one of them, where you might land! Watch out!"

I could not understand...as I had never seen anything before, so I just ignored it and continued dancing...

Soon after, my energy, and the energies around me, started to vibrate differently...like a big electric shock...and without seeing, I started hearing everything around me. I suddenly heard very loud howling sounds from afar! The cries embodied a being that was in agony! It was tortured, cruelly abused, unjustly enslaved...filled with guilt and resentment...it was begging for help! The screams were getting louder.

With so many different vibrations, messages and energies enveloping me, I realized that I had now landed in a different space-time reality. Evolving and changing to new patterns of energies, I transformed into all kinds of roots, trees, branches and leaves. Suddenly I got gifted with more complicated, three-dimensional forms of information in the form of smells, tastes and touches...so magical, and I enjoyed each and every one of them! I relished the gentle breeze...absorbed the kindness of the sun's generous brightness into my deepest cells and bloomed out happiness...flashed out enjoyment colorful and juicy. With all nature, I danced, celebrated and kept on chanting the "Word"! for all those wondering presents. After all, I was only a speck of dust bouncing in darkness before! We were all designed to "Serve" each other generously and silently...with "Love".

During all these amazing experiences, I would sometimes have wild attacks from one type of animal which was out of order! They were everywhere...breaking my roots, flowers and fruits! Most of the time, they did not appreciate me and took me for granted! They were demanding, cruel, arrogant, and thought that they owned everything! I felt their aggressive selfishness around me! I cried silently in pain, as these animals carelessly carved meaningless words on my body!

I started to evolve even stronger, and this time, I felt trapped in something all around me. Mystically guided, I started to knock these barriers down. It was very hard at first, but I did not give up...and as a result, I broke the wall. Immediately, a very bright and shiny light entered my being! I screamed out loud for the first time the "Word!" and got even more rewarded with floating life as fresh air into my body! So magical! Astonished by the beauty of this light and my new level of breathing experience, I started to break more barriers, and as a result, more light and excitement entered me.

I remembered that when I used to dance in the dark, I would think that it was the only world! I was now able to see all around me. What a gorgeous, gracious and glorious Heaven!

Enjoying being a part of this existence—this "Heaven," I continued to evolve, from a crow...to a dove...a parrot...a proud peacock and into over ten thousand types of birds...even the pure and powerful eagle! I flew over the heads of these wildest of animals that were hungry for power and control. They were taking away peace from everyone...living in limited stone boxes...with limited thoughts! They were like me...when I was just a speck of dust and thinking that was the only world!

One of my most horrifying experiences was when I was a chicken. I suffered great abuse from them. They populated out of control... they imprisoned, tortured, ill-fed, drugged and forced me to continuously lay eggs to fill up their hungry stomachs! They have been ruining the entire planet! Sure enough, their nasty actions would have equal and opposite reactions and consequences...!

Continuing evolving, I experienced being all types of animals and constantly suffering from being this animal with two legs. I remember being a little fish, swimming and dancing around happily when I was suddenly trapped in a net...then a harsh and sharp knife cut my throat. I was no longer afraid of the bigger fish since they would not kill relentlessly! We were all in tune with the intelligence, rhythm and natural cycles of the ecosystem... all but this wild and out of control, controlling and self-entitled monster!

While I was a peaceful and kind shark, playing my part in this moving masterpiece of heaven, they crazily and cruelly captured me, cut my fins, and threw me back to the ocean…I was in pain and agony…with detached vital parts of my body. These wildest of animals had an insatiable hunger for attacking, killing and cruelty. No other animal would do such ugly and nasty thing!

I never forgot the nightmare, when mountains of their self-made, hard, and poisonous hooks, nets and other objects, would stick in my mouth or neck, and entrap me, until I died! They also created a terrifying device that emitted a killer sound, vibration and fear! Millions of us died or became sick and the whole ocean became unlivable. I pleaded to God to destroy these arrogant beasts! Sure enough, their nasty actions would have equal and opposite reactions…and consequences!

I wish I could forget when my exotic and beautiful generations of various kinds, were completely and repeatedly killed and destroyed. Our skins were hung from inside the arrogant and proud boxes!

Another horrible experience was in the body of cows…forced fed …forced to produce milk day-after-day until death…to satiate their endless hunger! I was fed candies and became addicted to sugar. They tortured us by not allowing us to move around, and therefore provide more delicious and tender meat for their heartless appetite and their endless greed for more money. Sure enough, their nasty actions will have equal and opposite reactions and consequences!

Suddenly, I started to spin again, but this time it was very different. Sometimes it was much faster, with a lot of love and light around me, and sometimes, slow, dark and mundane. I experienced completely new feelings with more complicated and mixed frequencies.

First, all at once, I became atoms, molecules, cells, tissues, organs and the full body, and realized that we were affected by a "little voice" which was even dictating to our DNAs. My mother's "little voice" would change the vibration of her entire body, and consequently, would change the vibration of my cells and DNA.

I was feeling and hearing everything around me, including my own heartbeat inside and outside the womb! I heard them all...singing, prayers, kindness, forgiveness, jealousy, greed, resentment, anger, sexual situations, and withdrawal from addictions. I was being poisoned with chemicals directly or indirectly, through my mother's thoughts and words. All these were the creation of my "little voice" which was born with me!

In quantum physics, when an atom is observed by an observer, it appears for that observer. When the observer takes their attention elsewhere, the atom disappears. Similarly, when someone meditates and shuts down their negative thoughts (the "little voice"), they automatically connect to pure consciousness and observe the "Light" and "Love" through their third eye. Since the person observes it, it appears for them. Pure consciousness is "Unconditional Love" and "Existence" itself, and one of its attributes is..."Giving". So, through its "Light", it starts to give "Existence" to each cell...the cell radiates the vital "Existence Information", feels "Love" and becomes those attributes itself, and therefore starts to pass it on to other cells and so on.

As a result, the organs start to communicate with each other again, and the immune system performs its function, eliminating sick and dead cells, and consequently, the body "Heals." This could be viewed as each cell becoming a generous lover... and each starts "Loving" and "Serving" each another. (This is scientifically proven and shown in brain scans.) When darkness is removed, the brightness of the jewelry within appears instantly!

I call the third eye, the "True Eye"...as it can see beyond this three-dimensional reality, and it is the only organ which is "One" in the body and a symbol of "Oneness", representing the "One and only Love" within you!

Depending on the selection of our thoughts, a spiral of energy gets created...thoughts...actions...rewards...chemicals...hormones ...moods...habits...and, depending on the direction of the flow, either sickness or wellness results in the body and mind! When the focus is on "limited thoughts," the holistic "Loving" feelings disappear from one's body and mind, and the person becomes selfish and switches to survival mode. They start feeling anxious, fearful, jealous, lonely, angry, in pain, and they hurt. The more they focus on those "limited thoughts", the more sickness appears. The spiral of energy starts to move inwards and downwards, gets smaller and smaller, and eventually shrinks to "nothing", and the person either dies or commits suicide!

At any given moment, you are either rising and emanating the radiance of your jewelry within (upward spiral to infinity) and so experiencing "Joy", or more separation from pure consciousness by engaging in activities that are selfish or not loving to yourself or others. The ultimate goal of the "little voice" is to have you kill yourself! And why is this such a great sin by all holy ideologies? Maybe you kill or destroy that bright inner jewelry which is a flash from the "Source", or did you just kill a piece of the "Source"? – the "Source" that could create "Joy" and "Love"!

In contrast, when a person's focus is on their purpose, holistic "Love" and "Serving" start to feel like abundant "Love, Peace and Joy." The more they focus on "Love", the healthier the mind, body and soul become! The result is that their spiral of energy starts to move outwards and upwards, getting bigger and bigger, and continues to expand towards "Infinity!" And yes, there is no "death", but they experience "Existence" at higher and higher levels up to "Infinity!"

Suddenly, in a timeless manner, I became the human being, and all human beings throughout history, all at once, in the form of one body, mind and spirit. I was Adam, Eve and the storyteller... all kings, queens and beggars at the same time...the abuser and the abused...the rapist and the kid who got raped...the innocent on a death sentence...the judge and the dictator who ordered it. I was all of them from the beginning of time to the present moment and in the future...abusing myself, stealing from myself, raping myself, killing myself...all humans collectively, from the beginning till now and in the future are one body...one person that is going through the ongoing process of evolution, just like everything else in the world. The same concept applies to nations, races, religions and wars between the "voices.".... Millions of me were just born, and millions just died, just like cells in a body and stars in a galaxy!

I realized, loud and clear, that all humans collectively, are like that one body...each person, as a cell...each government, nation or country, as an organ. They need to communicate through "Light" and "Love." When darkness is observed, the "Light" disappears, communication breaks and "little voices" become loud in individual heads. Their "Light" diminishes, and therefore humanity as a whole gets sick, depressed and lost...the suicide rate just increased a second ago!

And the big bang! After any explosion, there is disorder and chaos, not incredible, stunning, self-organized and expanding "Breathtaking Miracles" right before our very eyes, are not for, or from, nothing! Each of them has a message. No one ever dies or is going to die and be "nothing", as energy never dies, it only transforms!

We can't measure and analyze something if we do not have access to its full dimensions. Therefore, we, as "limited" entities, cannot analyze or measure the "Infinite Being!" By observing its "Magical" creations all around us, and through meditation, we can open our "True Eye" and feel its "Infinite Love" and see a world with its true qualities. This "Loving, Holistic and Beautiful Intelligence" is behind everything! It does not matter what you call it and with which language. How about if we all call it "Love"? Would there be any more fights over right or wrong and over one "God"?

Every person is gifted with at least one talent, one opportunity or possibility to rise and shine in "Grace," and a purpose or mission to accomplish accordingly. Most of the time, however, we fail by giving away our beliefs and control to the "little voice", which hijacks our chance to reach the "Light" and experience real and lasting happiness and true "Joy."

As humans, we all go through so many challenges, and the bigger the challenge, the greater the reward! Mostly, the challenges are caused by our, or other people's, "little voices". Just like dust on a mirror, so are negative thoughts on the "True Eye". Every time, however, regardless of my pain, needs or difficulties, I chose to "Do" the "Right Thing." I learned, evolved, strengthened, and therefore "Awakened" more! As a result, I felt more "Love" and "Joy!" The quality of "True Happiness" is totally different, and no words from this limited space-time reality can describe it! It is like explaining the flavor of strawberry to someone who has never tasted it!

All matter and limited objects have expiration dates. They provide temporary pleasures in the beginning, but their quality diminishes in time...all the way down to "nothing!" They get old, out-of-fashion, rusted, broken, burnt, worn-out or ruined. They are also tools for the "little voice" to take a person down further and maybe forever – the ultimate goal of "little voice," just like drugs, which kill gradually. They are temptations for "death", in the form of manipulative, destroying and transitory pleasures...the energy of darkness, "death" and "nothingness!" The more done, the more miserable, crazy, and completely "out of control and under its control!" ...puppets of the "little voice!" They begin to lie, steal, sell drugs, kill, and eventually die for being slaves of the "little voice."

True "Joy", on the other hand, is exactly the opposite! It would never die, diminish, lie, cheat or get old. Every time you remember it, you feel "Joy", because it has the same frequencies of "Existence." Examples are when one helps or saves someone's or an animal's life, or everyone enjoys nature even if they see it a million times...like sunset, ocean or mountains. "Love" loves us so much that it created these masterpieces for soothing and caressing our eyes and souls! Or it could have created a big bang and made a big and ugly mess!

"Love" is the best thing to embrace and rely on! Like our best and only friend, it never puts us down, unless it is for our progress. It provides ease, confidence, security, peace and purpose! It is the "Healer"—whoever created the body, can also heal it! By meditating and touching the "Love" field every day, thousands of people are healing their cancer, MS, diabetes, etc.! We can either rely on and "love" a "limited" object that is conditional and eventually hurts us...or rely on the "Source" of everything and everyone. Therefore, love everyone and heal...then heal others! One is "limited and dependent" matter, and the other is "Unlimited Generous Unconditional Love", Beautiful "Free" will...and it is our choice!

TIPS ON HOW TO "CONTROL" THE "LITTLE VOICE"

The "little voice" is very smart, manipulative, realistic and logical. Ironically, it can be your coach...it never gives up. It tries all different ways until it gets you! It is extremely disciplined and works around the clock, even when you are sleeping. It starts small and eventually gets the whole world, one bite at a time! It knows the keywords and formulas of your "emotions". So read your manual before using it. Let us all learn about the most important organs in our body, the "brain and heart" and teach it in schools instead of sex! The "little voice" knows the brain and its habitual characteristics better than we do, and knows how to make you addicted!

The "little voice" controls " its emotions!" If you succeed by not listening to it, it will never give up nor show any emotions. Instead, it will wait quietly and watch your every step, and get you when your guard is down!

First, start to clean up negativity from the garden of your mind. One by one, monitor your thoughts, and catch yourself when thinking about memories from the "past" that do not empower you. Learn your lesson and move on. Be aware of distracting subjects that take your energy away from your purpose. You have a much more important mission to achieve! More importantly, do not fall from the "Grace!"

Open your heart to the "Light" and ask it for guidance to show your purpose. Prime yourself first thing every morning! Practice breathing techniques, meditation, gratitude, and decide how to be your best version and "Shine" your jewelry to the world! Accomplish your purpose with "Joy". Pass this space-time reality to a much more "Real" and "Higher" level of "Existence."

Feed the "little voice" with positive and "Light" materials on a daily basis. After all, "it" needs "Love" too! Soon "it" will start to follow you and give back the same progressive thoughts and feelings. Get addicted to "Joy!" It is the best addiction, and the side effect is "Healing"! If you do not have anything to feed it, and limited feelings start to emerge, immediately start practicing "Gratitude". Appreciate "it" and all the "challenges" in life for being the steppingstones for your "Fly!" It is well worth it, and you can handle more "Light", and be able to rise "Higher" and "Higher" to "Infinity!" Just like when I was inside the egg, the more I broke the walls around me, the more "Light" entered me!

We should all celebrate and marvel the "Brightness" and "Beauty" of this MAGICAL WORLD! What a gift! – Breathtaking... magnificent landscapes. What a masterpiece of perpetual creation in motion!

All of a sudden, a group of energies that were passing by, sent me a telepathic message: "There are other "Stunning" totally different, and more "Magical" worlds. "You" are now ready for the next!

I chanted the two "Magical Words!"

Author's Acknowledgment
To my beautiful father and my five grand grandfathers (all authors)

About Anahit

Anahit Etemadi is an inspirational leader, eighteen year TM practitioner, businesswoman, multi-dimensional artist and designer. Her passions are to empower women, inspire youth, help talented kids, stop sex trafficking and rescue voiceless animals. She has utilized her talent, experience, and education, to create her fashion brand, empowering women and men through fashion, while contributing to these important causes.

Anahit's father was a pure and spiritual person. He was enlightened, highly-educated and a deeply knowledgeable man. He was also very well respected and trustworthy in his extended family and community. He set the foundations of her belief system within her soul at a very young age, and without a doubt, is the main reason for her successes. He taught her that any talent comes with a responsibility to contribute back to society, so her purpose in life was formed at an early age.

Creating an international fashion line was a vehicle for fulfilling her spiritual path. Therefore, she moved out of the country – completely alone – with only a fair knowledge of the English language. In the past twenty-two years, she has lived in UAE, Canada and the United States. Initially, she had no family, relatives or friends in any of these countries, and as a result, Anahit has gone through tremendous amounts of intense challenges and difficulties, both financially and emotionally. However, she has never given up and kept persevering!

Anahit completed her Post Graduate Project Management program at Humber College, Canada, and attained the prestigious PMP Certification. She was then offered a scholarship from HULT International Business School, for which, she moved to the United States, and obtained her Master of Business Administration (MBA).

Awards
- "Award and Prize", "First year of primary school, Exceptional Talent Exhibition", for her female bride portraiture.
- "Honorary Diploma plus a full gold coin", "Museum of Contemporary

Art and Fashion" exhibition/contest, among professional and famous designers.

- "First Prize Winner", "Canadian and Italian Embassies in Tehran" fashion show and contest: "Shahrazad Goes to Milan."
- "Marylin Monroe Walks Nude", "Warner Brothers" and "Seattle Art Museum" one of a kind and masterpiece couture.

CHAPTER 8

USING EDUCATIONAL MARKETING TO BUILD RAPPORT, CREDIBILITY AND CRUSH OBJECTIONS

BY GREG ROLLETT

Everyone's favorite question to answer at cocktail parties, family reunions and networking gatherings is the infamous, "So, what do you do?"

Some people have it down pat. "I'm a personal injury lawyer," or "I'm a real estate agent."

Others, not so much. "I'm a writer…a blogger…and I help people manage the social web."

When we started the ProductPros, I found myself in the difficult position of trying to explain what it is that I do and how I help people in their business. Creating information products has a place at the forefront of the information marketing business, but not so much for nearly everyone else on the planet.

For prospects and potential clients, we had to take it a step further.

While they understand what an information product may be, the concept of "We'll build your product for you." is lost on many people. In comes the power of using educational marketing to help paint a picture in our prospect's mind as to what we do, how it can help them, and why we are the expert, and the company they need to hire in order to get the results they desire.

Throughout our marketing campaign, we do this in a variety of ways – from live and recorded webinars, where we place an emphasis on education for 60-90 minutes, to free reports and manifestos. We also use the media to leverage their audience to share our story and our message, providing education through print, TV and online media outlets.

One such outlet that we recently used to our advantage was working with Andrew Warner and Mixergy.com. Mixergy is an online publishing company that interviews successful CEO's and entrepreneurs in an effort to help other CEO's and entrepreneurs build successful businesses. Mixergy has interviewed the likes of Tim Ferriss, Gary Vaynerchuk, the CEO's from Kiva, Groupon, Wikipedia and more. And now, it was my turn to help out.

Our interview was focused on creating and developing information products, even if you are not a guru. The interview was actually constructed as a step-by-step system for building, recording and releasing a first information product. The interview with Andrew and I lasted about two hours and was the definition of using education to gain interest, trust and rapport with a community.

After the interview was aired, numerous viewers contacted me inquiring about my work. They loved the interview and the information that I shared. The interview built a bond with the audience, as they saw my face (it was a video interview), my passion and my voice. I gave them everything that I knew about the subject.

When you are free to give value to an audience, and you over-deliver through education and information, you can quickly gain control of an audience. There is something about being vulnerable that opens you up to bonding and trust. This type of educational marketing will quickly allow you to do three powerful things in your business:

1. Build Rapport With Your Audience.
2. Build Unmatched Credibility With Your Audience.
3. Crush Objections That Your Market Might Have about You and What Your Business Does.

In the Mixergy interview, I was able to do all of these three things through the education I provided in the content. The results from this interview alone have translated into thousands of dollars in new business from clients that had never heard of me before the interview. That is very powerful indeed.

Let's explore how you can use education in your marketing in each of these three areas:

I. BUILDING RAPPORT WITH YOUR AUDIENCE

Today, more than ever, people are constantly being hit from every angle with advertising, information, ideas and brands. New companies, solutions, advertisers and experts are popping up literally every minute. How can you not only grab their attention, but also connect with them emotionally, making them remember you and take the next step or action?

This is done through rapport building. Wikipedia defines rapport as: "The relationship of two or more people who are *in sync* or *on the same wavelength* because they feel similar and/or relate well to each other."

In other words, in your marketing, you need to educate your marketplace that you know your market better than they do. You need to make them feel that you are just like them, and that you understand them and that they can come to you when faced with a problem.

Education is the best way to do that. Think about your favorite teacher in grade school or high school – the one that opened your eyes on a subject. This teacher found a way to connect with you, to get past the bad feelings about class work, and actually got inside your head, got you to pay attention and take action (in that case, passing your exams).

You need to now do this in your marketing. A great example is from Chris Guillebeau and how he builds rapport in *The Art Of Nonconformity*. Chris has been blogging about his life and his business since 2008. It started as a place to speak freely about his quest to travel to every country in the world before his 35th birthday. He is now only a handful of countries away from accomplishing this goal.

Along the way, Chris has built an online and offline publishing business that allows him to live his desired lifestyle of travel and creative production (books, blog posts, training programs and events). As he began to build his tribe, he needed to create a reason for people to follow him. He had an incredible story to tell and a movement that would resonate with a global audience that wanted more from their existing lives.

As the blog grew, Chris wrote his *World Domination Manifesto*, which explained his story, his travel ambitions and his new outlook on what work and life should be all about. The manifesto instantly connected with thousands of people from all over the world who were now hung up on every word Chris wrote. They were hungry for more.

Chris then developed a series of "Unconventional Guides," his first suite of products for this audience. Had Chris not educated his market about his mission, inspired them through his own journey and ambitions, and let them into his world – essentially building rapport with a hungry audience – they would not be so eager to buy his "Unconventional Guides," to help elevate his books to *New York Times* Best Sellers, to purchase tickets to his sold out annual World Domination events and use his game-changing products.

The rapport he built is so strong and focuses on a 90% educational and informational strategy, and only 10% sales. The trust with his tribe is immense and is difficult to match in his marketplace.

In your business, you may not have the luxury of delivering 90% free and useful educational content, and that's okay. What you do need to do and understand is that you cannot underestimate the power of connecting emotionally with your audience and how they are feeling.

This can be a manifesto, a book, vulnerable blog posts, videos and even webinars or events where you can connect on that emotional level. That connection can be unmatched and can help you to build a loyal tribe.

II. BUILDING UNMATCHED CREDIBILITY WITH YOUR AUDIENCE

The second piece to educational marketing is showing your audience that you, and you alone are the sole expert that can solve their problem. You do this by educating them about your credibility in your marketplace. People today do business with people that they know, like and trust. They are buying you for *who* you are, not *what* you do.

Maybe businesses focus on the "*what*" part of their business – the features and benefits – that make their product great. While it is important to be great at what you do, you need to spend more time educating people on *who* you are. What is your core story? What are your values? What makes people connect to you on a human level?

In building unmatched credibility, you also need to educate people on what you have done and the results you have achieved for people just like them. Remember, in building rapport, we were able to connect with people on that emotional level. Now it's time to show them that you are the right solution for them.

People really do relate to things that they are familiar with. In knowing that, be sure to showcase your media mentions, major awards that resonate with your market, high profile people and businesses you have done business with, and other accolades that would draw the attention in the brain of your target client or customer. All of this plants the seed for credibility.

Now, we want to take it to that next level and blow them away with our ability to help them get results. People pay big money for results. How can you create educational pieces that drive results for your clients? When I talk about product creation I always tell my audience that you need to make the first step very easy and actionable and that will deliver near instant results for your audience. You don't want to do what I call the "P90X Pass Out Plan." This is where after seeing your material, or going through your program, they are so exhausted or overwhelmed that they cannot go on, take action or get any results because their mind or their body has been completely shut down.

One great example of using education to build credibility and ignite action is from Ramit Sethi's *I Will Teach You To Be Rich*. I love this example because Sethi has two major objections to overcome from the moment someone see his name or visits his website. First, is his ethnicity. American society is not accustomed to seeing or hearing from a guru with his cultural background. India is not seen as a country where you would want to learn about financial information. His second major roadblock is the name of his site and business. It sounds like a "get-rich-quick" program, which is far, far away from being the case.

In order to overcome these obstacles, Seithi created an amazing educational series that viewers can receive right from the homepage of his website. When you visit his homepage, you will see references to major media he has been featured within, and also a note about his New York Times best-selling book. This is an instant credibility booster. Then, instead of a traditional free report, which many people relate to (aka: *give-me-your-email-address-and-I-will-send-you-a-bunch-of-promotional-emails-to-buy-my-stuff*), Seithi is actually giving away the kitchen sink and then some. When you opt-in to his newsletter, you instantly receive content that is better than many expert or guru's paid content. It includes:

- The 80/20 Guide to Finding a Job You Love.
- The 30-day Hustling Course with interviews, worksheets and exercises.
- The Idea Generator PDF and MP3.
- Successful Client and Student Case Studies.
- The first chapter of his NYT best-selling book.
- and more...

...all of this just to get an email address. That is very impressive and one look into the material, and the credibility factor for what he does and teaches goes through the roof!

In your business, look for ways to over-deliver and drive results for your clients before you ask them for money. Showcase your credibility in a way that helps them to accomplish their needs and desires in life and business. Once you do this, the selling becomes superfluous.

III. CRUSHING PROSPECT OBJECTIONS

You can use education to advance the conversation in the head of your prospect to move them one, or multiple steps closer to choosing you as the person to help them solve their problem. You have seen that with the first two steps, building rapport and building credibility. Even if you get through both of these detectors in the brains of your market, they will still have objections and red flags floating around in their minds. This is where the third and final piece of the puzzle comes together.

Every day, you hear objections as to why people are not yet ready to buy your products or services. Maybe it is price or that they don't fully understand your offer. Maybe something is conflicting in their mind, or they feel they don't have enough time to put it into play. No matter their objective, you have the ability to educate them on why their objective is not the answer and that your solution is.

Having an objection to a product or service that your market needs really means that they don't have the right education as to how it will impact their life. Your job is to educate them by teaching strategic points that paint a vivid picture in their minds that you are the right man or woman for the job.

If you have gotten this far, I want you to spend a few moments writing down every objection that you have heard as to why someone is not committing to your product or service. Talk to team members, write things down on a white board or just make a list on a sheet of notebook paper.

Now think about stories, case studies and information that will help to overcome each of these objections. What does your customer *not know* that is causing them to say…"Not-right-now!"

A great example of overcoming objections in action is from Celebrity Press Publishing (CPP). Nick Nanton and his team put together a list of reasons people might not be using their publishing company. He turned those objections, or reasons, into a stellar report called, "The New Rules of Becoming an Author – The 7 Myths Of Publishing Success." When someone wants to learn more, or is raising one of the key points mentioned in the report, the team at CPP can instantly send over the report as a PDF or mail a physical copy via FedEx that they can see, feel and read to overcome the objections that they might be having in their minds.

Nick is using educational marketing to showcase his expertise and build rapport with the audience. He showcases his credibility by telling stories of successful authors and then crushing objections. This becomes a powerful sales piece that is used as marketing. Again, it allows the prospect to come up with their own conclusion that Nick and Celebrity Press is the right solution to help their business.

THE POWER OF EDUCATIONAL MARKETING

I hope you can see how powerful using education can be in your business. It allows others to make up their minds about what you do and how you can help them. Even better is that you get to create the message and the materials. You control the output.

And if anyone ever asks you again at a party or event what you do, you will now be able to educate them and help them understand who you are and what you do.

About Greg

Greg Rollett is an Emmy® Award-Winning Producer, Best-Selling Author and media expert who works with entrepreneurs and small business owners from all over the world to use media and marketing to create a business that fuels their life. He is the host of Ambitious Adventures, a travel reality show for entrepreneurs that can be seen on Amazon Prime and Entrepreneur.com.

Rollett is the founder of Ambitious.com, a media network that is known as "the voice of small business." Through Ambitious.com and the Ambitious TV Network, they have been able to create hundreds of online TV episodes and thousands of snackable videos for their clients that have been seen millions of times and have generated millions of dollars in sales for his clients.

Greg married his high school sweetheart Jennifer and they have 3 boys, Colten, Ryder and Ashton.

CHAPTER 9

FRAMING POSSIBILITY

BY MAY BAGNELL

When you change the way you look at things,
the things you look at change.
~ Wayne Dyer

LIFE

I was born with a disability. I arrived in this world broken. Literally.

My mother, a woman of stature at just 5'2", went into labor on January 15, 1968. I was about to arrive on the scene at a sizeable ten pounds! The birth process was not going to be easy on her. As was customary in hospitals, women in labor were given drugs to deal with the labor contractions. The combination of the medicine and my sheer size, proved to be too taxing for my mother. Her heart stopped.

Imagine the scene, she is pushing to deliver me and as my head was emerging she went into cardiac arrest. That labor room became an emergency room as teams of medical personnel arrived on the scene. Two lives hung in perilous conditions. Two women were fighting for their lives, together…one to start her human journey and one to continue hers.

Because her heart had stopped, everything else in her body came to a screeching halt including the womb that had been actively working to deliver me. As the one team rushed to revive my mother, another team raced to assess how to rescue me. My broad shoulders were trappedin her pelvis as her whole body went into lock down. The attending physician made the only choice that could save my life. He had to break my right clavicle. The procedure saved my life but it paralyzed my right arm. The function of my arm was absent as it hung limp.

Both teams were triumphant in the rescue of both of our lives. It was a day of receiving. We were both given the gift of this precious life – however rough the start had begun. My mother now was faced with a choice. How would she look at this situation? How would she see my disability? She made the only choice she could. She chose to see me as whole, to see me living the life I was purposed to live. She prayed daily…not that I should heal but that my disability would not hinder me from my God-given purpose and meaning.

Those early days were not easy as a young mother, but she chose to see the situation differently. She saw the possibility not the disability. She dedicated herself to my 24-hour care of feeding, diaper changing, soothing and physical therapy exercises prescribed by the doctors. She remained focused on what was possible for my life.

One day, when I was about 3 months old, she was going about her regular routine of caring for me. She had left me on the bed momentarily as she turned to get something. When she looked back at me, she thought she saw my right arm move. But of course, she thought, "no…that can't be…I must be imagining things." She had prepared to raise a daughter who knew no limitations despite her disability, but this? Could this really be happening?

That was a day of receiving the gift of a God-given miracle that the doctors had no explanation for. It was a day for receiving the gift of "seeing things differently" for both my mother and for me. While I regained the use of my arm, I was left with some restriction. But all these years, I have grown in gratefulness that I was the recipient of such a divine gift. My minor restrictions only serve as a reminder that *framing possibility shifts the focus from "what is" to "what could be."*

What about you? What do you believe is possible in your life right now? Your work? Your family? Where do you lack vision? Where do you need to shed some new light? Are you in a place of fear or doubt? Be encouraged my friend. What I am about to share with you can help you shift your focus no matter your situation. The truth is...*You have the power to create a whole new way of "seeing" any situation. You see...the truth is...how you "see" is how it will "be."*

LIGHT

Much of what has been made visible to me about my work as a life coach, I gained through my work as a photographer. Join me as I take you through a photographers guide to framing possibilities for your life and business.

When you change the way you look at things, the things you look at change.
~ Wayne Dyer

Vision

All my sessions, whether photography or coaching, begin with casting the vision for what we will create. We plan and visualize the mood and theme we are after. This is foundational for all that will be created. From there we are inspired to add the items that will enable the vision.

Harnessing a vision for your life or business is key to establishing a framework from which to create. Your mind has the ability to experience feeling a future event. Think of a time when you were preparing for a long anticipated vacation. Perhaps it was a beach vacation. The more you planned and prepared, you could just about hear the seagulls, feel the warm sand under your feet and taste that Piña Colada! *You can use the power of your mind to cast a vision for your life and business.* Vision boards, whether hand made or on Pinterest, are key tools used by successful leaders to see their desires already manifested.

Say: I am the co-creator of my life.

Lighting

So much can be said about lighting. While light is boundless, it can be harnessed to shed the appropriate amount of illumination for the subject, space and mood. The word photography literally means painting with light. Knowing how to be a light observer and how it falls on the subject will dictate the overall mood of the image. Where you focus your light relative to your subject will dictate the mood of the overall image.

In the canvas of your life, your creative tools are your thoughts and your words. They are the light sources you are casting to give form to any subject or circumstance you face. Do you look at your past with regret or longing? Every time you think, you can be shaping and illuminating your future.

Say: The past is a place of reference, not a place of residence.

Focus

For photographers, focus is the mother of sharpness and what you draw the viewer's attention to. Focus allows the photographer to highlight a particular aspect of the overall image and make it the star of the show. Without focus, the image is uninteresting, blurry and devoid of inspiration.

Situations in life and business can easily become blurry without the intended focus applied. However, there can be situations when you don't really want everything in focus. It can be distracting and overwhelming.

The lens of your life works much in the same way. *Focus on who you want to be in the circumstance, and watch your circumstance shift.*

Say: *I don't have to put everything in focus, only what matters.*

Composition

The composition of an image is all about how you want to have your subject appear in the overall frame. You have a host of possibilities... you can compose with your subject right in the middle, like all beginners will do, or you can master how to create a more interesting composition by training your creative eye. Either way, as the artist, you have the choice.

You have the choice on how you see any circumstance. *We all start at the beginner level but if you are willing, you can master how you see.*

Say: *The way I frame a circumstance has the power to change the circumstance itself.*

Depth of Field

DOF is used to emphasize part of the image or the entire scene to get the "big picture." In some situations, it may be desirable to have the entire scene sharp and in focus. However, if you desire to highlight only a part of the overall scene, "the details" for example, you utilize visualdepth to make the subject stand out. One way photographers can utilize DOF is by selecting the appropriate aperture of the lens, the size of the opening through which light can travel responding to the lighting conditions.

In our human optics, the pupil is the aperture. When you experience very bright light, your pupil responds and constricts to limit how much light is allowed in. In dim lighting situations, your pupil opens wide to allow as much light in for your ability to see. The depth of your perception is necessary for your ability to integrate information. At times we need to see the big picture, the full frame, with a clear view. And at other times, we benefit from focusing on the details.

You may find yourself in a "dark" scenario. Sometimes the "light" is nowhere to be found. However, you can control the amount of light you let in by remaining wide open to what is possible. You have the power to shift your visual depth to serve you and the circumstance at hand.

Say: In any given circumstance, I have the power to respond and remain open.

LESSON

Recently, my husband and I took a short trip to visit our youngest son. We spent some time together exchanging ideas. Our son is a philosophy major in college, so these conversations are certainly a source of great intrigue. All three of my children have been used to be great mirrors and teachers in my life. As we conversed, I shared my thoughts on framing possibilities and the importance of what you choose to focus on, and he shared with me Plato's *Allegory of the Cave*. Fascinated by this allegory concerning human perception, I felt it was an instant tie in to my thoughts.

When you change the way you look at things, the things you look at change.
~ Wayne Dyer

Imagine in your mind a dark cave. In the cave, three prisoners are held bound and cannot see anything except what is projected in front of them on a wall. They have been there since birth. This cave is devoid of light except for a fire that is burning behind them and the people carrying the objects which projects shadows on the wall—both of which theprisoners are unaware. To the prisoners in the cave, the projections cast on the wall appear real because, of course, if they have never seen the real thing, to *them*, that is that real thing.

One day, one of the prisoners escapes his dark existence of the cave. He is taken aback to discover what he "sees" outside his cave. As he gets accustomed to this world, he comes to terms that his previous view was only part of the reality. He is fascinated to see a much larger source of light: the sun. Content with his discovery, and with his mind expanded, he cannot wait to return to the cave and share this great news with the other prisoners. Much to his dismay, they do not believe him and shun him for even bringing such ideas into the cave.

As I reflect on this allegory, I cannot help but see the connection. We can easily get lost in the cave of our own thoughts and negative beliefs. Operate this way for long enough, and over time, the shadows of those negative beliefs become reality to you. That reality becomes all that is possible. *But what you did not notice is that you successfully fabricated a reality based on a very small source of light.*

The key to framing possibility is the willingness to shift your focus and use the appropriate light source to help you "see" differently. You can focus on the problem or you can choose to focus on the possibility. We unconsciously live by a certain way of seeing. *You have the power to choose.*

Practice framing new possibilities to shift you from where you are now to where you desire to be. Be brave and courageous to walk out of the cave of limitations into all of God's best for your life.

Desire to be Uncommon, because now you know – how you "see" is how it will "be."

About May

Becoming personally involved with each of her clients, the versatile visual artist, life coach and personal brand leader, May Bagnell, has created a powerful niche as an in-demand lifestyle portrait and brand photographer. When May tells her subjects that they've entered the "no pose zone," this is their cue to smile, relax and simply enjoy the moment. Her unique artistry will do the rest—and make every memory live vibrantly in the process. Her storytelling ability to capture visual poetry is evident as she documents the lives of her client's *life celebrations*, *brands*, and *dreams* through Personal Branding and Coaching that leads to inspiring documentary films and imagery.

One of the most fascinating aspects of this ambitious entrepreneur's emergence as a world-class photographer and coach is the unexpected, serendipitous way her lifelong passion became a busy full-time career. Growing up in Miami, she developed a love for photography and people from an early age, inspired by her physician father, who took the family on numerous trips for vacations and medical conferences and shot hundreds of pictures to chronicle their adventures. May's favorite photos were those that captured life's happy moments, catching people in joy and fully expressed – images that collectively told a story.

"The way it happened was like a dream come true for me," says May. "It's a career that is a joy to wake up to and do every day. Besides being personally fulfilling, the big payoff for me is bringing delight to the clients I am privileged to serve. My coaching work along with my photography work is very lifestyle-based. I'm always living momentto- moment looking for that spark and personality that illuminates the day and allows me to best help my client really "see" themselves. Looking back, one of the most serendipitous things about my life is that the act of helping women with the birthing process, in my early career as a birth coach, in turn actually birthed my career in life coaching. I discovered that I could nurture this dream and love every moment of making it come alive and grow over the years. I am a true believer that *everything shapes us*."

May, an International Coach and Photographer, has been mentored by some of the best in the industry. She has been taught by the Robbins-Madanes

Center for Strategic Intervention, Divine Living's Gina DeVee, Landmark Education and others. May Bagnell works with her clients to move past limitations, embrace what is possible and tell their stories in a compelling way.

A big believer in paying it forward, May enjoys speaking and teaching about her experiences as a photographer, entrepreneur and her journey with God. "My heart's desire," she says, "is to encourage others that there is a divine plan. Being a part of creating what's possible we can help budding dreamers achieve their goals. It's all about finding where that passion lies, and it's wonderful to watch other women like me grow into their own God-given dreams."

You can connect with May Bagnell at:
- may@maybagnell.com
- MBagnell@aol.com

CHAPTER 10

THE UNSPOKEN RULE YOU NEED TO KNOW

BY RICHARD SEPPALA

THE GREAT PYRAMIDS

In my many years as an entrepreneur, I have read countless books on how to be successful... I've even written a few. I'm not alone in this, because that's just what we do. As entrepreneurs, we are the risk takers of the business world – the Mavericks, the Speculators, and the Pioneers – setting out to explore new frontiers and achieve what has never been accomplished. We are often making it up as we go along. This means that there is no set rulebook for what we do, so when the trail we're blazing gets a little rocky, we gravitate toward the writings of those who have gone before us, in search of a little inspiration and assurance.

While the very nature of trail blazing means that we are heading in a direction that has not been explored, every good pioneer should gather as much information as he can from his seasoned peers concerning the proper gear to pack for the journey.

It's easy enough to find the needed inspiration and preparation advice... words we need to hear that tell us to believe in ourselves and follow our dreams... the ones that tell us to pack enough provisions to see us through to our destination. I believe these are words that we NEED to hear – make no mistake about it.

But what I want to talk about in this chapter is a topic that I feel doesn't get as much coverage as it should. This dark side of the entrepreneurial world exists, and bad things are happening all the time, but it's a subject that's rarely talked about because nobody really WANTS to hear about it. Why do I feel so strongly about bringing it out in the open? Because you NEED to hear it. You need to know it exists and you need to know how to recover from it. I'm going to tell you about my personal experience with both.

With my ROI Matrix software company, I am an entrepreneur in today's booming tech industry. This makes me the modernday equivalent of one of the old Wild West Cowboys or Gold Rush Pioneers. This is a pretty accurate comparison, if you really think about it. The tech industry is a HUGE mass of unexplored real estate, with products and services growing and expanding in all areas at a lightning-fast pace. Like the westward railroad expansion and the Panama Canal, the technology infrastructure has been laid to allow mass migration. However, like the Old West, while regulations have been put in place to govern the new territories, there are still plenty of places for nefarious outlaws and thieves to hide and simply not enough lawmen to flush them out. We all know there's gold in 'them thar hills', but we need to proceed with caution.

With all of that being said, what happens when your snakeboots fail and you're deep in the woods, when your compass and sturdy walking stick break, and when your carefully planned provisions get swept down the rapids of a rain-swollen river. What happens when the people you chose to make the journey with you turn traitor and take off with your horse in the night? What then?

Early in the development stages of my software company, I attended a tech conference. While making the vendor rounds, I met a young man who was selling a software platform. We had a great conversation and I was so impressed by his great presence and sharpness that I took his business card. Fast-forward several months, and I was finally ready to launch my new software platform. This was a labor of love for me…after a year and a half of design building, programming, and beta testing, I had developed a platform that could help change the face of online advertising.

With the planned launch scheduled for a large upcoming online traffic event, I began making preparations for how I wanted its presentation to go. I remembered the sharp young tech salesman and decided to give him a call. After another lively conversation, we both decided that I would pay for him to make the trip out and give things a trial run… see if he and ROI Matrix were a good fit for each other. His financial circumstances were similar to many young men just starting out… no safety net… so I offered him the hospitality of my home and my family made him feel welcome while we prepared for the launch. This first event was modestly successful, so with another event scheduled for two weeks ahead that presented even bigger opportunities, we agreed to extend his stay at my home until then.

During the two-week interim, we spoke often about work, life, and even relationships, with him seemingly regarding me as a mentor in these areas, even asking for advice on how to be a good step-dad to the son of his girlfriend. Four days before the scheduled event, he left for a motorcycle ride and didn't come home that night. I was unable to reach him and knew nothing of his whereabouts until he showed up the following day with 40 stitches, broken shoulder and collar bones. He claimed to have been hit by a drunk driver, and I had no cause to doubt his story, even though something in the way he told it seemed off.

In spite of his injuries, he attended the event with me, and it was a success, with many new sign ups and clients for the platform. Back home, with high morale and hopes for the future, I hired him full time as sales and account manager. When he moved inwith his girlfriend and began working remotely from his home, things took a downward turn. Instead of an increasing database, I began receiving reports from him that people were testing the platform, but needed things tweaked in order to be sold on it. If we could make those changes and extend the free trial period, they would be happy. I agreed, because after all of the work I had put into the software, I wanted it to be right for the customer.

Fast forward three months, and still no revenue brought in. This had me feeling pretty discouraged, and I didn't know how much longer I could continue to pay him a salary. I scheduled a meeting with him with the intention of putting him on commission-based pay but didn't get far enough into our conversation to do so. Shortly after his arrival, U.S. Marshals surrounded us and arrested him on the spot with an out-of-state warrant.

I thought this had to be some sort of identity mix-up or a paper trail error. Shortly after moving out on his own, he came to me hat in hand, asking for a personal loan so he could pay out-of-state parking tickets to make a fresh start. In my mind, I thought that these somehow hadn't been recorded as paid, so this was why he was arrested. It was all a mistake, surely.

It certainly was... MY mistake. He wasn't at all the person I had believed him to be, and I discovered this as I watched and read the press releases the following day. I won't tell that part of the story because it's not mine to tell, but I will say this. I jumped up and ran to the phone to begin doing damage control with our clients, before people read the news and began associating his name on the news with MY company!

This is where the story gets REALLY interesting. On my very first call to our free trial 'beta testers', I started by assuring the client that while the gentleman who had been our customer account liaison was no longer with the company, I would be continuing to fix the issues and honor the free trial extension... to which the client replied "What are you talking about?! I LOVE the platform – so much so that I just paid to attend the upcoming company retreat!"

One after another, this same or similar stories began stacking up... to the tune of over $400k. In case you are wondering, there was never a company retreat scheduled, and I was left with loads of angry clients, with no money on hand to refund them.

Yes, I took him to court. Yes, I won. But I have to tell you, the moment I left the courtroom instead of feeling relief and vindication, I felt the worst I have ever felt. I spent $60k in attorney fees to win a pile of debt and a piece of paper saying some jerk owes me a large sum of money that will never be paid.

I felt betrayed on a personal level by the man I welcomed into my home and family, who made a fool of me by pretending to admire my family values and look up to me, all the while robbing me and my customers blind. I was angry at him for his scheming and angry at myself for falling for it.

Let me take a moment to thank you for following along so patiently. I needed to tell you all of the layers of this story so you could understand the level of loss and betrayal I felt.

Now this is the part I want you to really take in and memorize by heart. To this day, people tell me that I should have closed shop and called it quits. Hung up my spurs and gone back East, if you want to go back to the Old Wild West analogy. There were times when a part of me wanted to, and it certainly would have been easier than what I did.

What I did was **I DID NOT** give up. I got up, dusted off my knees and my pride, and I got back to work. I worked tirelessly to salvage my company and repair my reputation. I didn't stop. I never gave up on my dream in the face of something much darker, much more painful than your run-of-the-mill setback.

In the beginning of my reconstruction, to say I was gun-shy would be an understatement, but the business world has no room for this. A few months of inaction is like years here. Sit still for even a moment, and your competition has forged ahead. You're also left behind, and spend precious time and money playing catch-up. This was not something I could afford to do, so I did one of the hardest things I have ever done... I took a steadying breath and forged ahead, no matter how scared I was of falling again.

This is that dark side I referred to. The fear, and how it can make or break you as a business owner. You simply can't have it. Not the kind that results in inaction, anyway. Whether it be anxiety over making the right decisions, or the bone-shaking fear of being bitten clear through your snakeboots again. You have to get up and make a decision. It might not be the right one. Odds are, it probably won't be, but that's ok. At least you made one, and the next decision you make will probably be better. And the ones you make that follow will be either the right ones or the wrong ones, but you will be moving forward.

The single most important rule to follow when working toward success as an entrepreneur is not to IGNORE the fear, but don't let it cripple you. Don't let doubts like 'what if?' or even 'what the hell am I doing?' bog you down and keep you from forging ahead. Bad things will happen, but even if they bring you all the way down to your knees, see it for what it really is... just a different perspective of the same forward-facing view, and keep on keeping on.

About Richard

Richard Seppala, also known as "The ROI Guy™," is an innovative marketing luminary, specializing in creating cutting-edge hi-tech systems, and is also a sought-after media expert, best-selling author and business consultant who helps companies maximize their profits by accurately tracking the ROI (Return on Investment) of their marketing efforts to the penny.

His newest hi-tech system, the Siphon (siphoncloud.com), utilizes revolutionary cloud technology to capture incoming traffic contact information, redirect that valuable traffic to targeted marketing and identify and protect you from click fraud, bots, malicious visitors and data thieves.

Richard founded his "ROI Guy" company in 2005. In addition to his acclaimed marketing tracking systems, called "The Holy Grail of Marketing," he also supplies businesses and medical practices with cutting-edge sales solutions designed to facilitate the conversion of generated leads to cash-paying customers.

By identifying marketing strengths and weakness, The ROI Guy™ is able to substantially boost his clients' bottom lines by eliminating wasteful spending on ineffective marketing, as well as leveraging advertising campaigns that prove the most profitable. By providing "all-in-one" automated systems such as his ROI Matrix (TheRoiMatrix.com), he offers real-time tracking of each generated lead.

Richard's best-selling books include ROI Power, *ROI Marketing Secrets Revealed* and *Marketing Avengers*. His marketing expertise is regularly sought out by the media, which he's shared on such high-level media platforms as NBC, CBS, ABC and FOX affiliates, as well as in *The Wall Street Journal, USA Today* and *Newsweek*. He recently spoke at the U.N. in New York on the topic of creating relationships and a unified trustworthy message with your marketing and is also a Fellow of Windsor Castle, having been selected as one of the 25 world leaders in shifting consciousness across the world.

www.ingramcontent.com/pod-product-compliance
Lightning Source LLC
Chambersburg PA
CBHW070818100426
42813CB00033B/3432/J